THE NEWER TEMPLES OF THE GREEKS

LEO ALLATIOS

THE NEWER TEMPLES OF THE GREEKS

Translated, annotated, and with introduction by
ANTHONY CUTLER

THE PENNSYLVANIA STATE UNIVERSITY PRESS

University Park and London   1969

STANDARD BOOK NUMBER 271-00076-7

LIBRARY OF CONGRESS CATALOG CARD NUMBER 68-8177
COPYRIGHT © 1969 BY THE PENNSYLVANIA STATE UNIVERSITY
ALL RIGHTS RESERVED
PRINTED IN THE UNITED STATES OF AMERICA
DESIGNED BY MARILYN SHOBAKEN

CONTENTS

PREFACE

The history of greece after the Turkish conquest has yet to receive the attention that scholars in recent years have devoted to the Palaeologan era and "the decline of Byzantium." Only the ecclesiastical aspect of Greek life has been investigated in any detail, notably by Sir Steven Runciman, "The Greek Church under the Ottoman Turks," *Studies in Church History*, Vol. II (London, 1965), and in the first chapter of Timothy Ware's *Eustratios Argenti: A Study of the Greek Church under Turkish Rule* (Oxford, 1964). Some particular problems of administrative and intellectual history are examined in T. H. Papadopoulos, *Studies and Documents relating to the History of the Greek Church and People under Turkish Domination* (Brussels, 1952). To all of these works the present author is considerably indebted; of each of these authors it can be hoped that some broader, fuller treatment of the period might follow their preliminary studies.

If post-conquest Greece has been largely neglected, cultural relations between Greece and Italy in the sixteenth and seventeenth centuries have been almost totally ignored. Almost alone in their field, D. J. Geanakoplos' *Greek Scholars in Venice* (Cambridge, Mass., 1962) and *Byzantine East and Latin West* (Oxford, 1966) suggest the importance of Renaissance intellectual connections between these two ancient centers of civilization.

The art historians have left this relationship severely alone. Yet the journeys of Greeks to the west—primarily successive emperors and their retinues—and the conquests of the Latins in the Levant obviously made more than a passing impact on the Italian imagination. When Piero della Francesca painted the Story of the True Cross at Arezzo, he depicted an early Christian myth; in the hands of Guido Reni, who continued the fresco series, the legend is converted into a notable essay in Byzantine history. Filarete's bronze doors for St. Peter's and Baglione's frescoes in the Pauline Chapel of S. Maria Maggiore reveal a lively interest in the personalities and problems of the Eastern Empire, which reached northern Europe with the arrival—if it did not occasion the arrival—of Rubens' tapestries on Byzantine themes. To my knowledge no historian of architecture has examined the relationship, if any, between the centrally-planned Greek church and similar schemes which took Italy by storm in the late fifteenth and sixteenth centuries.

In short, intellectual connections between the two countries have been generally disregarded and a key figure in this relationship, Leo Allatios, quite overlooked. To many his name is known only as it is attached to hundreds of pages of translation and annotation in Migne's *Patrologia Graeca*. Some of the reasons for this neglect are not hard to discern. His Latin is of the densest Renaissance variety and his passion for citing authorities makes slow reading of his works. Many of them are, however, of intrinsic philological interest and, in the present translation, I have preserved most of the sources that he cites in the footnotes. Retained, too, are those quotations which have an immediate bearing on subjects which he discusses. Those citations which merely serve to confirm an already documented observation I have suppressed.

If Allatios' ecclesiastical and architectural terminology seems at times improper to the Byzantinist, it must be remembered that he wrote the two letters which make up this book as one Catholic to another. For this reason he often translates freely into the language of Rome concepts that are purely Greek. Where his terminology is especially remarkable I have again tried to draw attention to this fact in a footnote.

I have taken the liberty of restoring to the author his Greek name, even though he lived the greater part of his life in Rome and signed in Latin or Italian most documents that survive. Although he was a devout Catholic, he thought of himself as a Greek. One instance must suffice in proof of this. In his discussion of the *hierateion*, the altar-enclosure, in these very personal letters to Jean Morin, he writes "no other place is designated with this name by us." All the while a member of the Roman Church, he distinguished between race and religion and, in doing so, seems consciously to have set his face against the contemporary political attitude of the Turks for whom the Greek people were represented only by their church and patriarch.

Allatios' Greek I have left "uncorrected" since it provides some interesting clues to the nature of the language, its accentuation and orthography in the seventeenth century. In translating the Latin, I have taken the opportunity to correct some misinterpretations of the text included in an article of mine on the *De templis* in *The Journal of the Society of Architectural Historians*, XXV (1966).

Finally I must acknowledge the encouragement and advice I received from Sir Steven Runciman and the help of Professor Douglas Stewart of Brandeis University in unravelling some of the more tangled knots in Allatios' prose. The Research Committee of Emory University and the South-Eastern Institute of Medieval and Renaissance Studies both generously supported the project. Without their help it is doubtful if this first version of Allatios in English could have been made.

A.C.

University Park, Pennsylvania

I
LIFE AND WORKS

SINCE AUTOBIOGRAPHY was not one of the many literary genres to which Allatios turned his hand, we have little information about his earliest years.[1] He was born on the island of Chios—in 1586 or 1587. At the age of nine he was taken to Rome by his uncle, Michael Neuridis, to study at the Greek College of St. Athanasius. The college seems to have rejected him as too young and Leo spent four years in Calabria and Naples before being admitted to the school. This rejection must have surprised Neuridis, familiar with the workings of the College from the ten years that he had spent there[2] before joining the Society of Jesus and returning to Chios as a teacher in a mission school.

The young Allatios came back to Rome in 1599 where he defended his theses in philosophy and theology eleven years later. He returned to Crete where he had been preferred as vicar-general by the Latin bishop of the island. Perhaps dissatisfied with provincial life, he returned to Rome where, in 1616, he took a degree in medicine at the Sapienza. This discipline seems to have appealed to him no more than life on Chios, for he immediately returned to St. Athanasius as Professor of Rhetoric.

Academic intrigue, especially the rivalry of his fellow Greek Matthew Caryophillis, forced him to withdraw and Allatios took a position as *scriptor*

---

1. The fullest account of Allatios' life is that by Stefano Grado of Ragusa, his contemporary and friend, ed. A. Mai, *Nova patrum biblioteca,* VI² (Rome, 1853), v-xxviii. For a briefer version, see L. Petit's article, *s.v.* ALLACCI, in *Dictionnaire de théologie catholique,* cols. 830–3.
2. *Cf.* J. Krajcar, "The Greek College under the Jesuits for the First Time," *Orientalia Christiana Periodica,* XXXI (1965), pp. 109–10.

in the Vatican Library. In 1622 Gregory XV assigned to him the responsibility of transferring to Rome the vast Palatine library offered by Maximilian
of Bavaria to the Holy See in return for the continued subsidies he received
from this source. Allatios arrived back from Heidelberg in June 1623 with
196 cases of manuscripts and printed matter.[3] For more than thirty years he
supervised this collection, producing in this period the bulk of his theological
and polemical writings. It must have been with some misgivings that, at
the age of 75, he abandoned this comfortable position to accept Alexander
VII's request that he become Custodian of the Vatican Library. Whether he
enjoyed this eminence or not we do not know. Certainly none of Allatios'
works bears a date between 1661, the year of his appointment, and his death in
1669, although his annotations to Syropoulos' history of the Council of
Florence, published posthumously in 1674, may have been a production of
this last period.

The range of his scholarly interests and talents almost defies description.
His published works include an early treatise on Etruscan antiquities (Paris,
1604), biographies of illustrious Romans of his own day (Rome, 1633), and a
commentary on the fable of Pope Joan (Rome, 1630). More seriously he
produced translations of Proclus Diadochus, many of the letters of
Demetrius Cydones, and George Acropolites' invaluable *Chronicle* (edited by
I. Bekker, Bonn, 1836).

Byzantine history seems to have been one of his passions for, apart from
his translations, he edited a variorum edition of the *Chronicle* of Constantine
Manasses (Paris, 1655), and an extraordinary essay distinguishing Michael
Psellos the philosopher from four other Byzantine worthies with the same
surname. This is the only original work of Allatios to receive the accolade of
inclusion in Migne's *Patrologia Graeca* (122, cols. 477–536). Why the editor
preferred this to Allatios' most celebrated work, *De ecclesiae occidentalis atque
orientalis perpetua consensione* (Cologne, 1648) remains a mystery. But the fact
that a book such as the *Diatriba de Psellis* was necessary is an interesting index
to the state of later Greek studies in the middle of the seventeenth century.

3. On this mission, see H. Lämmer, *De Leone Allatii codicibus qui Romae in bib. Valli-
celliana asservantur* (Freiburg, 1864).

Allatios' reputation, so far as it exists, is as an antiquarian and a polemicist. He has been described as "violent against the Greek Church."[4] Certainly little violence is in evidence in the works devoted to a liturgical and physical account of the Orthodox rite and its architectural setting. The *De templis Graecorum recentioribus* and *De narthece ecclesiae veteris* (Paris and Cologne, 1645) are sympathetic accounts of Byzantine worship rather than polemical tracts. A lesser man would have used these opportunities to deride the church which he had abandoned. Even his *encheiridion* on that bone of contention, the Procession of the Holy Spirit (in Greek, Rome, 1658), contains more gentle admonishment based on scholarly objectivity than vituperation.

It was perhaps this gentleness which secured for him the respect and love, as well as the scholarly admiration, of many of the leading Catholic divines of his time. Preeminent among these was Jean Morin (1591–1659). Hailed as "the most learned Catholic of the seventeenth century,"[5] Morin had been born a Calvinist but converted to the older confession at the age of nineteen. His authority in historical matters was appealed to many times by General Assemblies of the French clergy and his *Histoire de la délivrance de l'Eglise Chrétienne par l'Empereur Constantin* became a standard work on ecclesiastical history.

In 1640 Morin was summoned to Rome by Urban VIII to aid in bringing about the union of the Greek and Latin churches. He became firm friends with Allatios. Their mutual antiquarian interest and concern for the Pope's ecumenical purpose resulted in a correspondence lasting several years.[6] This dealt in the main with problems arising from the practices and terminology of the Orthodox rite, its buildings and their decoration, vestments and service books. Allatios' two most important letters on these subjects make up the *De templis* and constitute the first systematic treatment of later Greek architecture and the liturgy which it sheltered.

An extraordinary sympathy of purpose and interests characterizes this

4. M. E. Cosenza, *Dictionary of the Italian Humanists,* I (Boston, 1962), p. 134.
5. *The Catholic Encyclopaedia,* Vol. X, p. 570.
6. Morin's letters to Allatios are collected in P. Desmolets, *Mémoires de littérature et d'histoire,* Vol. I (Paris, 1749), pt. 2.

correspondence. The combination of mutual affection and scholarly rigor is strongly reminiscent of the friendship between Erasmus and John Fisher, bishop of Rochester, two centuries before. Fisher requested, but did not live to receive, a Latin translation of the Greek liturgy. Morin asked for an *explication du texte,* complete with an elucidation of Byzantine architecture as it reflected pristine Christian traditions. The exposition makes a worthy counterpart to Erasmus' excellent translation.

But Morin was not the only scholar who turned to Allatios for help. Gabriel Naudé (1600–1653), librarian to Richelieu and Mazarin, sought enlightenment about the plethora of Greek liturgical books—the *euchologion,* the *heirmologion,* the *tetraevangelion* and so on—so many, as Allatios says in his response, that they could not be read aloud in the course of a year by a man who devoted himself exclusively to this task.[7]

Even after his death Allatios offered what must have seemed an inexhaustible mine of information to European scholars. Jacques Goar, the great French liturgist and editor of the *Euchologion sive rituale Graecorum* (Paris, 1647), depended much on the Greek savant's work. In his annotations to Cedrenus, for instance, reprinted in I. Bekker's edition of the historian (Bonn, 1839), Goar frequently acknowledges the *De templis* as his authority. Allatios' book, written forty years before Du Cange's indispensable *Glossarium ad scriptores mediae et infimae Graecitatis* (Lyons, 1688), is identified as the source for much of the French scholar's information.[8]

The reason for these tributes is not hard to discover. Allatios offered these early Byzantinists not only an unparalleled knowledge of the medieval Greek sources but, more importantly, what gave life to this erudition—a prolonged and profound acquaintance with the Orthodox rite. Although a devout Catholic, he had enjoyed the indispensable experience of being born and raised in Greece. And even when he rose to a commanding position in the intellectual hierarchy of the Vatican, he did not turn against the culture and faith of his homeland.

Nearly always Allatios' writings evince a pride in being Greek. He deals

---

7. *De libris ecclesiasticis Graecorum dissertationes duae* (Paris, 1645), pp. 3–4.
8. Cf. *Glossarium,* cols. 196, 378, 963, 1622 and *passim.*

far more roundly with the heretical Protestants than with the merely schismatic Orthodox. This is apparent in most of his nineteen books[9] and even more strongly in the many more works which have not passed beyond the stage of manuscript. One of these, the notes on Sophocles written in his maturity and preserved in the British Museum, reflects more than the obligatory seventeenth-century concern with antiquity. It is a deliberate and loving attempt to elucidate the early days of a continuing tradition which no amount of Turkish harassment could efface.

9. For a complete bibliography, see A. Calogierà, *Raccolta d'opuscoli scientifici e filologici* (Venice, 1728).

II

GREEK ARCHITECTURE AND WORSHIP UNDER THE TURKS

BOTH BEFORE AND AFTER the fall of Constantinople the Turks dealt much more leniently with their conquered Christian subjects than conquering Christians—filled with the zeal of Reformation and Counter-Reformation—did with one another in western Europe. The horrors of the religious wars of the sixteenth and seventeenth centuries were known to Allatios at least by report and it is probable that he thought them fully justified.

The Ottomans, for centuries the only Turkish tribe possessing a common frontier with Christendom, considered their encroachment upon the west a holy war. But they could not and did not treat the *Romaioi* as pagans, for the Christians were a "People of the Book" and their Lord a Prophet of Islam. They therefore could not be persecuted nor converted at sword-point and, as long as they remained submissive to their political overlords, they might worship undisturbed.[10]

Allatios' native island had lived under Turkish domination for a generation by the time he left for Italy and the picture that he draws of this subjugation is not harsh. Orthodox and Muslims had an established *modus vivendi*: Turkish troops would even protect Greek religious processions from harm and their women, albeit secretly, provided oil for the lamps that burned before icons in the churches. Such toleration is only partly to be explained by the Turks' innate respect for piety. It was also an act of policy as Sir Paul Rycaut, English consul at Smyrna in 1678, realized:

10. Timothy Ware, *Eustratios Argenti. A Study of the Greek Church under Turkish Rule* (Oxford, 1964), p. 2.

> The Sultans . . . in the Conquests of the Grecian Empire judged that
> a toleration of Religion would much facilitate the entire subjection of
> that People.[11]

Rycaut's testimony, and that of many other western residents and travellers
in the east, amply confirms the moderate attitude of the Ottomans suggested
by Allatios.

This moderation, applied almost universally in ecclesiastical affairs, was
almost totally absent with regard to political liberties. The Greeks enjoyed
very limited opportunities for education. Apart from the Patriarchal Academy
at Constantinople, only Jannina, Patmos, and Chios possessed schools where
the Christian tradition might be studied. Again, if these *gymnasia* were few,
printing presses were totally denied to them until the middle of the eighteenth
century. The colophons of books by Greeks in the seventeenth century are
marked Venice, Leipzig, and Vienna, but never Athens or Constantinople.

Another type of harassment more clearly reveals the workings of Turkish
policy. Between 1625 and 1700 there were fifty patriarchs of Constantinople.[12]
The Sultans made an enduring, if small, profit out of Greek ecclesiastical
rivalries and this simoniac acquisition of offices by the great is an interesting
counterpart to the manner in which humbler Christians obtained permission
to build, or rebuild, their churches. The first chapter of the *De templis*
describes the ubiquitous recourse to bribery without which this sacred
construction could not continue.

The importance to the Turks of revenue from the Greek Church is
laconically suggested by Rycaut in his treatment of the monks of Mount
Athos who

> pay a Rent to the G. *Signor* of a thousand dollars a Month, which is more
> in my opinion than it could have been let out to Turkish farmers on a
> rack Rent and is the best improvement the Turk could make of it.[13]

That such fees were paid is, of course, as much a tribute to Greek faith as it is
to the conquerors' fiscal ingenuity.

11. *The Present State of the Greek and Armenian Churches, Anno Christi 1678* (London, 1679),
     p. 21.
12. Ware, *op. cit.*, p. 4.
13. *The Present State of the . . . Churches,* p. 220.

The English consul compares the suffering of the Church to the Passion of Christ, suggesting that the former could be endured because of the latter's "Grand Exemplar." This Christian persistence, in fact, seems to be due to the fact that the Turks did not interfere with the Orthodox liturgy. If the Greek Christian had this, he had all. Left with the central *mysterion* of his faith, he might endure anything. The number of post-Conquest martyrs is considerable, but the divine service continued to be celebrated.

This is not to suggest that the Greeks could exercise their religion in complete freedom. Rycaut tells of

> the subversion of the Sanctuaries of Religion, the Royal Priesthood expelled their Church and these converted into Moschs; for such I have seen in Cities and Villages, where I have travelled, rather like Vaults or Sepulchres than Churches, having their Roofs almost levelled with the Superficies of the earth . . .[14]

A Christian dome or tower might not compete with a minaret, although there is no body of legislation in which to find such a restriction. The *ad hoc* nature of Islamic law allowed the Turks an almost unending trickle of venal income. But it also permitted churches to be erected throughout their Greek possessions. Nowhere did this pious building flourish more than on Chios.

14. *Ibid.*, 11–12, quoted in part by Ware, *op. cit.*, p. 3.

III

CHIOS AND ITALY

> Now the Ancient Structures and Colleges of Athens are become ruinous and only a fit habitation for its own Owle, and all *Greece* poor and illiterate, such Spirits and Wits amongst them are forced to seek it in *Italy*; where sucking from the same Fountain, and eating bread made with the same Leaven of the Latines, it is natural that they should conform to the same Principles and Doctrines.[15]

Thus Sir Paul Rycaut describes the state of Greece in 1678 and indicates one reason for the diaspora that so sorely weakened Greek intellectual life. But this cannot suffice as a total explanation, for the island of Chios, which probably enjoyed more spiritual liberty and material prosperity than any other formerly Christian part of the Turkish empire, suffered a similar exodus. Allatios was but one of many Chiots who responded to the magnet of Italy,[16] the new center of classical studies now that Greece was in bondage. Here scholarly controversy flourished and the Greeks, even before and long after Bessarion, found exercise for their minds in polemics concerning the perennial questions of philosophy.

The Byzantine mind, after the ecumenical councils, had shied away from theological precision. This disinclination to define had been one of the principal vexations suffered by the Latins at Ferrara-Florence; the rejection of most of the Council's decisions by the Greek people must have convinced many Italians of the Greeks' incapacity for logical thought, whereas, in truth, it represented only the Byzantine apophatic tradition. Freed from a theocratic environment the Greeks were as ready as any nation to enter into

---

15. *The Present State of the . . . Churches,* pp. 28–9.
16. For a partial list, cf. J. Krajcar, *op. cit.,* pp. 107–11.

debate: classical philology, the literature of antiquity and of the Fathers, cosmology, mathematics, medicine, law, all could now be discussed more or less freely in their chosen exile.

By the sixteenth century, Italy was ready to receive these emigrés in considerable numbers. The Greek College of St. Athanasius, where Allatios both studied and taught, had been founded at Rome by Gregory XIII in 1576. Particularly during its period of Jesuit administration, the College served not only the Greek Uniates but also acted as the training center for proselytizing missions returning to Greece. Other Italian academies, such as the Orthodox College at Venice, seem to have been less interested in making converts. At the universities of Pisa and Florence the respective merits of Plato and Aristotle were debated by the exiles at least as urgently as the virtues of leavened or unleavened bread. And Greeks sat at the feet of Protestant masters at Halle, Paris, and Oxford as willingly as they listened to Catholic professors in Italy.

To these students life in Greece offered only intellectual censorship. On Chios alone did some measure of freedom of thought exist.[17] It is no accident that the majority of Greek pupils at Venice and Rome were products of the *Chia Skolē* where Latin and Italian were taught in addition to the subjects in the traditional *quadrivium*. This freedom extended to ecclesiastical matters. The "ancient Capitulation made with *Sultan Mahomet* the Second," of which Rycaut speaks, was a set of special privileges ensuring religious liberty as well as a sizeable number of "civic liberties."[18]

The influence of Rome was strong and the Jesuits, Capuchins, and Dominicans all had schools on the island. Yet this did not make for intolerance. Rather, intercommunion was a common practice, a point made by Allatios to support his thesis of fundamental agreement between the Catholic and Orthodox faiths.[19] Latin bishops were permitted to celebrate

17. That intellectual freedom does not necessarily result in intellectual achievement is a point made by Rycaut in one of his more sour observations on the Chiots: ". . . a wise man is as rare amongst them as a green Horse."

18. P. P. Argenti, *Chius Vincta, or the Occupation of Chios by the Turks and their Administration of the Island* (Cambridge, 1941), pp. 208–27.

19. *De ecclesia occidentalis atque orientalis perpetua consensione* (Cologne, 1648), pp. 1659–62.

in Greek churches: lack of such forebearance could only have created strife on an island many of whose leading families were of Italian origin.

From 1304 to 1329 and again from 1346 to the Turkish conquest, Chios had been under the control of the Genoese. Although the colony withstood the Ottomans until 1566, its mother city refused military responsibility after the fall of Constantinople. The island was left to its own devices and, in this comparative independence, religion and the economy both thrived. As late as 1694, the year in which the Venetians occupied Chios at the invitation of its Latin population, a French traveler recorded more than "200 Christian churches . . . at least 30 convents of men and women, both Latin and Greek, that carry out their worship without molestation of any form."[20]

Although he had left Chios at the age of nine, Allatios seems later to have been aware that in his homeland there remained perhaps the most flourishing branch of Greek civilization. To elucidate this civilization, to communicate to others its traditions, and to discover the root common to both the Latin and Greek churches was his life's work. His purpose and his achievement emerge most clearly in his works on the liturgy and its architectural setting.

20. Quoted in P. P. Argenti and S. P. Kyriakidis, Ἡ Χίος παρά τοῖς γεωγραφοῖς καὶ περιηγηταῖς, Vol. I (Athens, 1946), p. 498.

IV

ALLATIOS AND THE LANGUAGE
OF ARCHITECTURE[21]

SIGNIFICANTLY ALLATIOS BEGINS his first letter by distinguishing the Greek
architecture of his own day from both the pagan temples of ancient Hellas
and their early Christian successors. He suggests no date or period as the
dividing line between the *templa vetera* from his *templa recentiora*: his correspondent had asked him not for an historical account but for a description of
contemporary Greek practice in the light of its liturgical and architectural
antecedents. But Morin and Allatios understood that the disputes between
the eastern and western churches were in some way reflected in the develop-
ment of their different rites, buildings, terminology, vestments, and manner
of sacred decoration. These differences arose when the Church had organized
and proliferated. No such schisms could exist in that pristine age when
Minucius Felix could say of his community, *"Delubra non habemus, aras non
habemus."*[22]

Allatios' procedure is to lead his reader from the monastery grounds into
the narthex of the church, through the naos, and finally to the bema. This is a
leisurely journey for extended digressions are made, protracted discussions
of social and economic conditions, the nature of the priesthood, and the
imperial prerogative. These are intended to illuminate the reasons why
particular features in the church are as they are. From the first, the modern

21. For a more detailed treatment of specific architectural features that Allatios describes—
as opposed to his descriptive language which is examined here—cf. A. Cutler, "A
Baroque View of Byzantine Architecture," *Journal of the Society of Architectural Historians,* XXV (1966), pp. 79–89.
22. *Octavius,* cap. 32 (*Patrologia Latina,* III, col. 53).

reader cannot fail to see that what we would call church furnishings—bells, benches, curtains, lattices, and the utensils of the eucharist—are of vastly greater importance to him than the structure or aesthetic aspect of the building that houses them.

His method is strictly textual and he may be counted as the first to apply this Renaissance technique to Byzantine architecture. He examines the way in which the Fathers and the historians, St. John Studios and Codinus and many others, have used a certain word and compares this usage with the interpretations that other seventeenth century commentators had laid upon it. Only then are the function, shape, and size of the object considered. The number of corrections he makes, the number of educated guesses in the *De templis* that turn out to be correct is a tribute to this technique.

On one occasion alone—when discussing the numbers of doors leading into the later Byzantine church[23]—does he record an architectural feature of his own observation. Not a shadow of archaeology darkens these pages, for, in 1643, archaeology was far less precise a science than philology. The fact that he had not seen Hagia Sophia at Constantinople does not restrain him from making repeated reference to particular aspects of the Great Church. In the last analysis, it is experience of the liturgy, not experience of the site, that concerns him.

But his correspondent seems to have demanded descriptions of specific types of churches. And it is in these descriptions[24] that Allatios' powers seem most sorely tried. He had to provide Morin with a vicarious experience when his own knowledge of many of the types was limited to what early Christian and Byzantine writers could tell him. The result is often an imitation of an imitation but none the less interesting for that.

Throughout Allatios appears incapable of sensing or, at least, of expressing the sensation of a three-dimensional form. He employs planar concepts such as *semicirculus* to convey the volume-defining idea of *hemisphaera*. Phrases such as *ambitu descrescente arcuantur* are used almost desperately to suggest the shape of a vault. It is possible that Allatios found Latin an awkward language

23. Cf. p. 34, *infra.*
24. Cf. pp. 25–29, *infra.*

for this sort of description. But ancient writers such as Vitruvius do not seem to have suffered from such restrictions.

Conceptual rather than linguistic limitations suggest themselves as the source of this difficulty. By the seventeenth century, an inability to describe a three-dimensional space seems almost innate in Greek writers. To understand the change that a thousand years had wrought, it is only necessary to compare Allatios' account of the *troulla* of Hagia Sophia with Procopius' classic passage on this church (*De aedificiis*, 1, 1) or the Church of the Holy Apostles (1, 4).

This inability (or reluctance) to describe masses and volumes has an interesting and more celebrated parallel in the history of painting. While the "flatness" of middle Byzantine decoration may well be due to an elaborate theory of how the icon functioned *vis-à-vis* the spectator,[25] the post-Conquest painter was certainly unable to render a form in real space. A footnote of Gibbon's reveals much about the Greek attitude towards the achievement of Italian Renaissance art:

> "Your scandalous figures stand quite out from the canvas: they are as bad as a group of statues!" It was thus that the ignorance and bigotry of a Greek priest applauded the pictures of Titian, which he had ordered, and refused to accept.[26]

Whether or not Gibbon's anecdote is apocryphal, it aptly illustrates the attitude of the Greek mind of the sixteenth century towards spatial reality. And Allatios' text confirms the impression that this mental disposition was not confined to artists. He thinks in terms of movement in two dimensions. The liturgical procession moves from the altar to the prothesis, into the aisle and back through the gates of the bema; churches are classified either by their ground-plan, or by their vault or roof type, but never by combinations of these features. Space is either horizontal or vertical but never an extension in volume.

This is hardly to Allatios' discredit. He ranks as the earliest writer to attempt any systematic description of Orthodox sacred buildings. And,

25. Cf. O. Demus, *Byzantine Mosaic Decoration* (Boston, 1948), *passim*.
26. *The History of the Decline and Fall of the Roman Empire*, cap. 49 (Modern Library edition, III, p. 5, n. 14).

ultimately, it was this quality of *sacredness* that concerned him. Beyond his importance in architectural historiography, he was the first to understand the extraordinary interpenetration of architecture and liturgy. That this was the unique achievement of Byzantine civilization is the meaning and importance of the *De templis*.

THE NEWER TEMPLES OF THE GREEKS

De templis Graecorum recentioribus

THE FIRST LETTER

To Jean Morin, most learned in and worthy of Antiquity

I

Most judicious man! I have to tell you not about those huge structures which Christian piety built when the Empire of the East ruled, nor about those sumptuous basilicas or temples raised by the skilful citizens of ancient Greece, but about those which the faithful secretly erect under the most bitter servitude and oppression of their religion, and those which destructive time has ruined that are yet cherished, venerated, and frequented.

With the divine cult in so much contempt, it is truly extraordinary how great a number of temples survives. In these the Greeks offer their prayers to gracious God himself, despite the wicked barbarism of the Turks who have published laws, with grave penalties, that no new house of the Lord may be built. Nor may those collapsed with age or destroyed be rebuilt without the decree of the governor. Doubtless these pious men, determined souls with a common purpose, need an immense amount of money to extort permission from the magistrates and the unkindly laws to repair churches now crumbling and collapsing. Often they are allowed only to buy a new building the size of a church now almost destroyed. But in this way their piety continues and suffices to maintain the divine cult.

Thus everywhere in Greece at this time, as I have just said, a great number of temples is to be seen. However, these do not have one type of façade common to all, nor are all interiors the same. They vary both in workmanship and decoration according to place and opportunity and the abilities of the builder. Some are small, rough buildings; others are made of the humble soil; still others may be despised for the meanness of their walls and wood-work.[1]

But however they are made, they do not lack for veneration. Frequent meetings of believers accomplish the divine liturgy in a manner that you may consider not unbecoming. The beauty of the perfect temple is restored and solemnly, on feast days, the offices of Christian piety are celebrated.

II

As the nature of the site allows, a broad and level group appears in every direction. The temple rises in the middle of this: it is pleasant to go around it and take advantage of the view. The ground is laid with stone or brick but fully open on all sides. There are no walls to obstruct and no fortifica-tions. One sees only the monastery buildings and the paths connecting them. These buildings enclose the area in the manner of a theater. One tree, of the kind that does not shed its leaves, shades the earth, protecting it from the heat of the sun with wide-spreading branches.

In the cities and places that men frequent guard is kept with fortifications joined, where possible, to the nearest walls of dwellings. You will see how different is the wall of the church made of the image of Christ, of the Blessed Virgin, of some saint or other—usually the patron saint of the church—painted above the door but also in its niches, in the hollows of the wall in every part of the structure. These icons are usually in the higher parts of the building but are sometimes attached to marble columns. Here is protection from airy creatures and other harms.

III

We have delayed long enough with externals; we will talk elsewhere of the church's porticoes. Proceed. But before you enter, consider the arch above the portal, decorated in various ways and with different types of speckled marble and, what is more magnificent, supported by columns and charmingly adorned with small cubes of mosaic. Beneath the arch are marble benches. If you are tired from your journey or the heat of the sun or if you wish to revive your soul with fine conversation or learned discourse, this seat will be most apt. Nor let escape you in one part an iron weight in the form of a sheet —I might say an iron leaf—and the iron hammer used by the λαυσπάκτης, 'the summoner of the people' (although in the typicon of St. Saba[2] it is the κανδηλάπτης, 'the kindler of the lamps or candles,' who does this. It could be that these two duties were combined, for often one person performs both duties. In his *Carmina*, Theodore of Studios seems to tell the chief canon to "sound the trumpet or strike the wood at the right time as is necessary").[3]

This sheet he strikes so that its noise falls on those who seek the temple to celebrate the office of divine praise. But these are signals to consecrated men. They are summoned to God not as the crowd in the cities but with only a single sound,[4] and that a great one, as Balsamon grandly expounds in his published meditation on the subject.[5]

Bells were in use amongst the Greeks, at least in recent times, as I learn from many sources but especially from the history of George Pachymeres who mentions them often.[6] When Byzantium was taken, the empire plundered, and the remaining sovereignty of the Greeks seized, the use of bells in the cities in which they lived was interrupted. The Turks feared that the sound might strike fear into wandering souls and destroy the peace which they enjoy.[7] Thus these raving men, this most trivial of people, philosophized about the soul. The priests, therefore, use a wooden instrument to summon the Greeks to church. The wood is twice ten feet in length, two fingers thick and four broad, neither split nor cracked, and best hewn with an axe. Holding the middle of it in his left hand, the priest or someone else strikes it rapidly, now in one part now in another with a wooden mallet held in the right hand. He hits it first near and then far from his left hand, now high, now low, in such a way that the well-aimed blow produces the sweetest music.

This is called the σημαντέριον, or rather χειροσήμαντρον since it is held in the hands and struck with them. It is different from another, larger instrument called the μέγα σήμαντρον which is hung with iron chains from its edges in turrets or bell-towers. This is of remarkable size, as much as six hands broad, one hand thick, and more than thirty in length. I remember hearing once from Athanasius, archbishop of Imbros, a worthy man and a good friend of mine who placed novices of his order on Mount Athos, that on the *sēmanterion* of the Dionysiou monastery is written this song, admittedly rude and barbarous: "Where are you from, o wood? I was in the middle of the forest; then I was cut down with an axe and taken away. Now I hang in the house of the Lord. The hands of pious deacons touch me and, when struck with the hammer, I emit voices, so that all may come to the temple of the Lord and find remission of their sins." The wood from which it is made is called by the corrupt name σφενδάκη which is none other, I believe, than the σφένδαμνος of Theophrastus, the maple of Pliny. We know that the use of wood of this sort is very ancient.[8]

These sacred pieces of wood are used in processions and on other occasions. Bells of brass or copper are very rare in Greece unless the town in which the Christians live is far removed from traffic with the Turks.[9] But there are many very old bells on Mount Athos and timepieces which, without help, tell the hours by the noise they produce. I have often heard from that same Athanasius of another type of bell which might truly be called clamorous.[10]

If I seem to have confused the σήμαντρα of the Greeks with the βαρέας, as the Greeks call them, these *vareae* should be thought of as similar to our bells but not exactly the same. I can explain this difficult point in a few words. If the *vareae*, as I say, are both struck with iron and at the same time emit a great metallic sound, they must be made of something other than iron.[11] If the matter is considered closely, these *vareae* are not bells but the clappers of the bells. They are called so since they are set in motion with a heavy, aimed blow.

Apparently the bells sound in three different ways. The first is a continuous sound made by contracting and relaxing the outstretched arm. The second peals frequently and loudly, although not without modulation. The third, struck with a hammer, makes the brass bells sound with individual beats. The *vareae* are nothing but the clappers of this last type of bells, struck heavily and separately.[12] When these have finished, the appointed time for the office is at hand. All waiting is ended by these blows on iron or wood.

IV

The part under the arch connected with the street, which you have called the *impluvium*, should properly be called the προαύλιον or πρόθυρον τόυ ναόυ. This is the vestibule of the temple. Zonaras calls it also the *propylaion*: τὸ γαρ πρὸ τῆς ἀψίδος πρὸ τὄυ προπυλαίου εστί.[13] Note the word apse used with this meaning. They used to call the middle of the atrium, or of the impluvium, μεσαύλιον or μεσίαυλον. Thus Cedrenus, writing of the thirty-seventh year of Justinian's reign, says "the fire burned the middle of the impluvium, which is called the *garsonostasion*."[14]

V

Enter. You are now in the pronaos. As Nicetas Choniates says "there in the vestibule of the temple whatsoever monk that enters prostrates himself and exposes his neck to be trodden upon."[15] First there is a chamber of the temple separated from the sanctuary by porticoes on all sides. This chamber is not connected with the sanctuary save by three doors—the middle one large, those on each side small. This part of the church is called the νάρθηξ by some writers who place it outside the church.[16] It is frequently mentioned in the ecclesiastical books of the Greeks.

You will also see that very many churches are not content with a single narthex, but have a second adjoining. In the towns, this is the place intended for women, in the monasteries for those monks who have not yet entered holy orders. They remain here since it is not permitted for them to enter the interior of the church while the divine liturgy is celebrated. In this spot, too, the bodics of the dead are placed while rites are performed for them before they are committed to burial.[17] Here also stand the penitents.[18] Some writers see the narthex as outside the church not because it is a separate place, but because it is separated from the church, properly speaking, where the priests have their place. These penitents were the ἀκροώμενοι who used to hear the holy scripture standing throughout the reading of the Gospel.

I do not dispute that in the ancient temples the narthex was perhaps outside the church. Nor that it could be said to be outside the church because it is different from that place which is rightly called the church. But about the narthex in our day, Gabriel Corinthius has aptly said "it is called the narthex where the women stand in the church."[19] However, the narthex is really neither the church, nor separate from the church, but contiguous with it. Otherwise how could those who were outside the church hear the scriptures read inside near the bema? Others call the προνάος the *protemplum*—that is, in front of the temple since it is not the temple proper.[20] Accordingly the place outside the "beautiful gates"[21] is rightly called not the temple but the protemplum. Nicephorus Blemmydes, in his Life of St. Paul Latrensis, used the elegant metaphor ἐν χρῷ τοῦ ναοῦ, "the skin of the temple."[22] For in the same way that the skin sticks to the living body and yet is not flesh, so the narthex is attached to the temple and yet is not the temple. The narthex, outside or in front of the church, is situated in the manner that we have described. This is as manifest as they are mistaken who maintain that the narthex was the door of the church in which stood the penitents of the second class who were permitted only to listen. These were the χειμαζόμενοι, those vexed with unclean spirits.[23]

VI

As has been said already, the narthex was connected with the temple by three doors—the middle door very large and most beautifully adorned, those on either side small and inconsiderable when compared to that in the middle. The middle door was also called ὡραία πύλη, the beautiful gate.[24] Thus the νάος, the temple in which the Emperor used to stand, is between the beautiful gates and the gates of the sanctuary. The beautiful gates are also called βασιλικαὶ πύλαι.[25] These are different from the holy doors through which one enters the bema. The holy doors are beyond the basilican doors, the beautiful doors between the narthex and the naos. The beautiful gate is also called Angelic.[26] Certainly this name could not be given to that of the bema, since entrance into the bema is denied to women.

The beautiful door is covered with a curtain which, always partially unrolled, marks the entrance. However, when the troparia are sung in the narthex during vespers or during litanies, the curtain covers the doors. These troparia and the midnight office—which they call μησονύκτιον—as well as

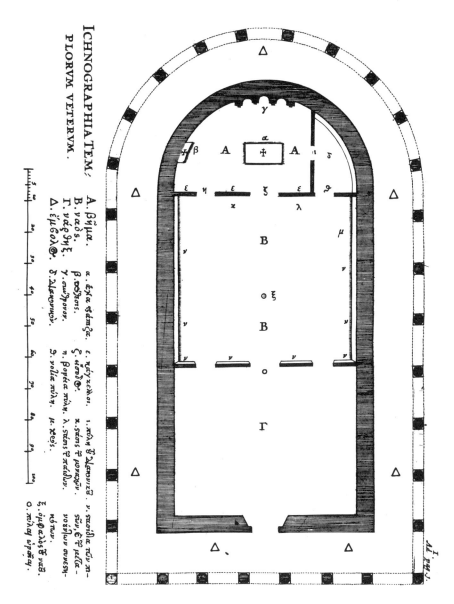

Fig. 1. Leo Allatios, *De templis Graecorum recentioribus*
(Cologne, 1645), plate I (*photo:* Emory University
Library).

the hours of terce, sext, and nones, they say in the choir with the doors closed. The first hour after matins and the ἀπόδειπνων, which is after supper, and compline they say with the curtain unrolled. Only the abbot[27] of the monastery, or a deputy substituting for him, stands. The rest of the monks remain at their benches in the naos. When compline is ended, all leave. But when the *mesonyktion* is over, the curtain is rolled up and the abbot and priests go into the naos through the beautiful door, the remaining monks—if there are any— through the lesser doors. When the hours are finished and the curtain of the beautiful door and that of the bema are raised, the priest standing in this entrance to the bema ends the office.

VII

This is the temple proper, called by some the choir. So that this vaulted space may contain as many as possible there are stalls attached to the wall, made of nut-wood or pine or other commoner boards. On these the priests rest, either in a sitting or a standing position, the more worthy and notable deservedly occupying a seat. The nearest stall is to the right of the beautiful door upon entering. These stalls, or *accubitoria*, are usually called τόποι or, more aptly, στασίδια.[28]

VIII

The middle of the temple is called the ὀμφαλὸς, the navel. Thus in Euripides we find ὀμφαλὸς γῆς[29]—Delphi, which was believed to be the middle of the world. So, too, in Homer[30] and Pindar.[31] Others have called it by the more correct name of μεσόναον.[32]

IX

Another vaulted space, longer than it is broad, crosses that of the choir. On both sides of the choir up to this new level you will find the singers who serve the office by reciting and chanting. Some call this space the *diaconicum*[33] —I do not know if rightly.

The board-work of the bema screen is entered through two, sometimes through three doors. The middle door is more beautiful, larger, and more dazzling in the grace of its construction. The side doors are less remarkable; they are covered with a curtain which must be raised before entering. The middle door is divided in such a way that the lower part is made up of two lattices or little gates which meet in the middle. These are less than the height of a man. The upper part is covered with a curtain and, while the offices are being recited in divine service, is seen quite openly. The curtain is rolled up and the gates exposed. These are only closed by the priest upon entering or leaving, or by the deacon when ecclesiastical business demands. When this is done is evident from the Greek books.

According to the 14th canon of the Laodicean Council, access for communion is permitted only to the priests.[34] The 69th canon of the Trullan Council prohibits any layman from approaching the altar with the sole exception of the Emperor when he wishes to offer gifts to the Creator.[35] Women are especially banned from it, although Balsamon observes that "in the regions of the Latins, women may approach the altar without shame whenever they wish."[36] Balsamon rails at this fact and does so with perverse hatred and out of ignorance of things Latin. For it is so that among the Latins women enter the bema. Where is the harm in it? Did not women enter the bema in ancient times, as Balsamon concedes?[37] Notwithstanding the manner in which women enter the sanctuaries of the Latins, where is there a people without sanctuaries?[38] He writes, without understanding its significance, that whoever wishes may freely enter the sacred shrine of the famous temple of Our Lord Jesus Christ in Chalcis.

X

Much is cleverly invented by Zonaras and Balsamon concerning the imperial prerogative.[39] Zonaras asserts that it is not permitted the Emperor to enter the altar as a layman but on account of the supreme power invested in him and recorded in the ancient writings of the early Fathers. The canon in question, he says, invested the imperial title with supreme power. Balsamon declares that since the emperors advance patriarchs by invoking the Holy Trinity they are anointed of the Lord. Not only when they made oblations, therefore, but whenever they wished, was it permitted for them to enter the

sacred shrine of the temple without impediment and to seal with the triple
seal in the same way as popes.

Someone has attributed this privilege to Greek flattery. This seems to be
true. Since all suppose that the emperors, with the increasingly sycophantic
approval of the court, were allowed to enter the shrine at will and be seated
while the mysteries were celebrated, the ecclesiastical order was thus reversed.
Ambrose moderated this arrogance and assigned a place to the emperors in
front of the chancel. In this way the Emperor, in the majesty of his power,
might sit first in rank but near the people. The priests, whose place was in
the sacred shrine, would precede him. And this was approved by Theodosius
and affirmed by his successors, especially in the reign of Theodosius II.[40]
Sozomen in his *Ecclesiastical History* tells us that this tradition was preserved.[41]

Nicephorus Callistus adds that Theodosius himself diligently followed the
prescriptions of Ambrose.[42] When on feast days in Byzantium he entered the
divine house and brought gifts to the "mystical table," he immediately
retired backwards. Nectarius questioned this behavior. Theodosius replied
that he perceived a difference between the emperor and the celebrant and
found Ambrose to be a true teacher and worthy of the episcopal dignity. If
the Greek flattery is dead that saw the Trullan canon as an agreement who
then, long ago as the fathers relate, set his foot inside the sanctuary? From
the beginning, Christian emperors entered the shrine to make their oblations
and afterwards withdrew to the outermost atrium leaving the sacred precinct
to the priests and to consecrated men.[43] However, the bishop or the priest
in the performance of his sublime duties, entered through the ἅγιας θύρας,
the holy gates. A large number of doors in the church may be praised in this
way, but only one is "holy" in the way that we have spoken of the "beautiful
gates"[44]: beautiful either for their magnificence or to increase their venera-
ability or to acknowledge their chancels which are many. This is a fashion
to which the Latins are not unaccustomed.

Concealed with veils and lattices, sacred shrines were no less secret from
princes and magistrates than from other men. In the *euchologion*[45] the veil
is called the βημόθυρον.[46] The lesser door to the north the euchologion calls

βόρειον κλίτον or πλαγίαν, to differentiate it from the little door to the south which is not found in all churches.

XI

The area enclosed by the bema screen is venerable and sacred. It may be entered only by the clergy, rarely by secular men, and never by women. Cantacuzenus calls it the shrine in his *Histories*. The Greeks more often call it the ἅγιον βῆμα, the holy tabernacle—what you have called the *sancta sanctorum*. In the euchologion it is the ἱερατεῖον.[47] Thus: after venerating the icons εἰσέρχονται τὸ ἱερατεῖον. No other place in the church is designated with this name by us. Clearly those who confuse the ἱερατεῖον with the choir are mistaken: those duties which are performed in the choir cannot be accomplished in the sanctuary and vice versa. That which it is lawful to accomplish only in the choir and that on which the light of Christ shines is unlawful if performed in the sanctuary. The choir is open to all Christians, the sanctuary only to the priests and clergy. These leave the choir for the sanctuary and there the celebrant takes his place because he may not do so in the choir. Whoever wishes may gather much information about Greek ecclesiastic affairs by studying their holy books. The typicon of St. Saba calls the *propitiatorum*, the place in which sacrifices are offered, θυσιαστήριον[48] and ἱλαστήριον.[49]

XII

So greatly venerated is this place that the name of his rank comes to the consecrated ecclesiastic from it, as though from something most potent— οἱ ἀπὸ τοῦ βήματου are those who, having advanced to the priestly rank, serve at the altar, make sacrifice at it, and celebrate the divine liturgy.[50] And therefore he is called πρωτοπαπᾶς, as it were πρῶτον τῶν ἱερέων, first among the priests. This name and that of the τάξις τοῦ βήματου, the priestly order, is in Gregory Nazianzen's oration on St. Basil.[51]

XIII

In the bema two altars, sometimes three, are set up. Where there are three, books, vestments, and other utensils are placed on the one to the left as you leave the sanctuary. In some churches, however, the area is separated from the rest of the bema by a middle wall or by paneling and is connected with the bema by an opening in this wall. Entrance to the bema is gained by a third door to the south in the paneling of the bema. Whether the place is separated by a wall or is one with the bema, this door is open only to the ministers or their assistants, for all men of this sort using it offer their service to the celebrants. When this place is separated by a wall it is called the παράβημα,[52] that is, a little place adjoining the bema. When a small building is joined to a lavra it is called παραλαύριον. Παραπόρτια means lesser doors beside a larger one; παρακλήσιον or παρεκκλήσιον mean a small shrine next to a larger temple; and so on.

The parabema is provided with a table and benches on all sides so that the servers, commonly called deacons, or *diacacia,* or readers[53] may set out the things necessary for the celebration of the mass. Some call them διακονηταὶ.

In this place are lighted the coals which are brought to the altar to burn incense. Here sacred cauldrons are filled with coals so that, as is the custom, boiling water may be poured on the chalice at the right time. Lighted candles precede the Gospel when it is carried to the ambo to be read and sacred offerings are solemnly carried from the lesser altars to the holy table—what is called the μεγάλη εἴσοδος, the Great Entrance—before they are consecrated. After consecration they are finally returned to the small altar, the πρόθεσις,[54] so that whatever remains of these gifts is taken by the priest or the deacon. The crumbs of bread, which they call the ἀντίδορον,[55] are kept for distribution to the people. Wine and dishes of food are set before the hoarse singers and the exhausted assistants.

This place is now called the diaconicum since here remain the ministers, the attendants, and the servants at the altar. Lest these attendants, who are for the most part young and ready for a game, do some absurdities and start some sport, there is an overseer for them—ὀπὶ τ'ἱερᾶς καταστάσεως, *praefectus sacro consistorio.* In Greco-Roman law and according to Gretser,[56] he is called *praefectus sacrae stationi*. This I would more properly translate as "master of ceremonies" or "director of the sacred rites and orders." In later Greek, κατάστασις means not a man's status, but his condition, his customs, his bearing, and his manners.[57] They call a man ἀκατάστατος not if he has no standing, but if he is shameless and conducts himself foolishly. When the Greeks see someone full of discretion they say, admiringly, ἴδε κατάστασιν or σύστασιν. Again, ταξία means not so much good order as proper and pleasing comportment while its opposite, ἀταχία, suggests an unaccommodating manner.

There the ὀπὶ τῆς ἱερᾶς καταστάσεως is stationed in the sanctuary to check youthful vigor and the boys' immoderate behavior. He authoritatively restrains their hubbub and squabbling and brings them back to the path of dignity from insults, disputes, and unseemly acts. Does this not satisfy you? Let us call him the prefect of the rite, seeing that it is he who watches over the divine liturgy so that it is carried out according to the precepts of the saintly Fathers. He sees to it that no one sets a foot beyond the prescribed bounds.

XIV

I do not know for what reason they call it the diaconicum—that place we call the sacristy, or *sacrarium,* where the ministers put on the sacred vestments for divine service[58]—other that in our day there is among the Greeks no sacristy adjoining the church. Today Greek priests and deacons are vested in the bema. Nor do I know if it seems more solemn when the bishop or some other priest is decked with the sacred vestments in the middle of the choir by the other celebrants. It was certainly different in the time of the early church as the 21st canon of the Laodicean Synod shows. This taught that it is not necessary for the ὑπερέται[59] to be in the diaconicum nor to touch the Lord's vessel. Yet how prevent them from entering when men of a lower station and even those who were the most contemptible of that time did so? Therefore the canon suggests a place more sacred and venerable than the diaconicum, and especially if by the term *hyperetai* the canon means those subdeacons whose duty it is to handle the Lord's vessel. One thing that was in the minds of the Council of Fathers, I believe, was precisely what the commentators, Balsamon and Zonaras, suggest: that by diaconicum the canon intends not a place but a function. Thus the lesser ministers should not undertake those duties which belong to the deacons.[60] It is not right for one man to discharge the office of deacon and that of candle-snuffer. For just as a priest cannot lower himself to an inferior order and thus violate his rank, so too the ministers, who are inferior to the deacon, cannot carry off the deacon's greater dignity.

Everyone must preserve his proper dignity and rank and accomplish his day's work in right order. And this is clearer if for Διακονείῳ we read Διακονικῷ as other manuscripts have it.[61] Nor does it hinder this understanding to read in the lives of the martyrs by ancient writers that he was buried ἐν τῷ Διακονικῷ, as I noted the day before yesterday in the elegant *Life of St. Artemis* by John Monachus.[62] This implies that they buried the bodies of the martyrs in the diaconicum as if it were a more holy place than we now consider it to be.

XV

The diaconicum is also called the μεσατώριον in the euchologium. This is perhaps the μιτατώριον of Theodore the Lector.[63] I think the word is a corruption as very often happens with foreign words and terms of this sort. Properly it should be μινσατώριον from the table (*mensa*) set up in the diaconicum for things to be laid out on it. The Greeks also use μινσύλια[64] and ἀντιμίνσια.[65] The word might come from μίνσον which denotes a dish. It is not surprising if from such dishes or other eatables which were kept in the diaconicum, as we have described above, this location should be called the μινσατώριον and later corrupted into μιτατώριον or μεσατώριον.

What *mitatorium* might be, Xylander[66] freely confesses in his notes on Cedrenus that he does not know. "Perhaps it was, as it were, a profane part of the temple," he says, "and admitted those who were prevented from using its sacred parts." It is not to be wondered at if among heretics part of the temple is considered profane, because for them the entire temple is so. For us Catholics the temple has several parts to it: so it is for the Greeks who respect the temple more than do the heretics. He adds something of which, on his own admission, he is ignorant. "What was done in the church of antiquity, I will not argue, since it is clear that among the light-headed Greeks a thing is repeatedly changed." Who is more light-headed here, Xylander or the Greeks themselves? The Greeks have followed the oldest Fathers and Councils. To these they have clung assiduously and the sacred buildings, in which they worship, have been venerated for many centuries. Xylander denies the faith of the most holy Fathers which has been affirmed by the blood of martyrs and confirmed by the opinions of many of the most excellent doctors. He defiles that faith, changes it and mixes with it the newest fancies of those—whom I know not—in his native land. For this reason he hates as profane and hinders understanding of the most holy places and the parts of these places. But why wonder at such raving against sacred buildings, when profane men, in their most profane languages, have distorted the Author of such buildings, reduced them to profane service, and cast Him down from the throne of majesty and holiness.

XVI

In the bema itself there are two altars. In the lesser one to the north the πρόθεσις, or, as you would call it, the *praepositio,* is performed. The name comes from this ceremony. In this chamber, before the mass, the priest and one of his assistants prepared everything which is necessary to complete the office, such as bread, wine, and so on.[67] This done, they withdraw to the central altar which is larger and adorned more richly. This is called the ἁγία τράπεζα, the holy table. After invoking divine aid, and as though starting anew, they begin the mass. They leave the prothesis by the little north door singing and carrying lighted candles already prepared before the mass. With the singers stilled, they go to the middle of the church and pray for the people's good fortune. This is followed by the Cherubimic hymn sung by the choir. The priest and his assistant take up the candles, reenter the great door and return them to the holy table. There the candles are deposited and the rite continued. When this is ended, what is left of the eucharist is carried back to the prothesis where it is consumed by the ministers or the priest.

XVII

In this same sacristy, the body of Christ, most precious to the sick, is weighed out and reverently preserved. Depending on the decision of the priest, it may be kept not in a place apart but in the wall. Sometimes in a miserable little church it is honored neither with torch nor taper.

It seems to me worth while to explain briefly the manner of its preparation. In the prothesis on the fifth day of the week the priest customarily separates the largest part of the fresh bread from the other pieces.[68] It is the custom in Greece, as well as elsewhere, to mark this piece with the sign of the cross. The priest venerates it, covers both this and the other pieces and takes them to the main altar for consecration.

When he takes communion, he consumes one-fourth of the bread and crushes the remaining three-fourths over the paten.[69] Although this may properly be done with fresh bread, he crumbles into dust ageing bread that has lost its moisture. He separates these particles, covers them and reverently completes what is left of the mass. The Greeks call these particles μερίδας,[70] but more commonly, and in the liturgy of Chrysostom,[71] μαργαρίτας. The piece which is cut from the body of Christ the priest puts in the chalice. This is called the pearl (*margarita*). So, too, by Clement of Alexandria.[72] The Greeks could not find a more appropriate name to indicate the body of Christ among similar particles.

XVIII

After noon the priest returns and, after much prayer, carefully takes the venerable *margaritae* from the paten. He places them in a vessel made usually of wood, but, where possible, of silver or gold worked after the manner of a pyx. They call this vessel the μιξόμηλον—a corruption, I believe, since they should say πύξόμηλον. Evidently from *pyxis* a bad form was produced. In antiquity the pyx was called the κιβώριον, a name which seemed good to many. Thus the ode of Theodore of Studios on the *ciborium* of St. John the Precursor.[73] Now, the later Greeks call it the ἀρτοφόριον,[74] the name used by the euchologion for the consecrated bread preserved, when it is not used up, for another mass.

XIX

Finally the paten is wiped with the *musa* lest any crumbs should remain in it. The μοῦσα is a piece of sponge,[75] compressed so that its holes are blocked. During the rite it is held in the fingers by means of a little silken string attached to one side of it. Mention of it is made in the euchologion, in the liturgy, and in the typicon of St. Saba; in Chrysostom's mass it is called simply the μοῦσον.[76] And just as the sponge with which the altars are wiped is called μουσιτοτράπεζο, so not inappropriately we call ἀρτομουσίτο that sponge with which the crumbs of bread are collected and the paten wiped.

XX

The *pyxomelum* is carefully enclosed in a piece of silk cloth or a small bag and reverently kept in the wall with lamps hung before it. These lamps are dim in comparison with the church. They are called ἀκοίμητα, since they never sleep, but keep a perpetual luminous vigil, or ἄσβεσα, inextinguishable. When the *pyxomelum* has been put in the wall and candles lighted, the priest accompanied by the deacons chants psalms and other hymns. Then he enfolds it in a wrapper and proceeds through the church to the houses of the sick and dying.

On the way, the Turks, should they encounter it, are amazed at this veneration. Do you by chance wonder that they are amazed at such great veneration? So that there is no reason for astonishment, I will dwell on this matter. In the city of Byzantium, and in others under the same domination, after a certain hour all night travel is forbidden. Only the prefects and their retinue are allowed on the streets—not for recreation but to restrain the lawless upon pain of punishment. When there is need, the priest and deacons do not wait for the dawn but with great ceremony carry the sacrament to the sick.[77] If the prefects meet them on the way, the cult so greatly moves the Turks that they see fit to ignore the regulations about being abroad. One of the Turks sets out with them, leads them where they wish, conducts them back to the church and, if necessary, to their own homes to protect them from molestation and attack. The Turkish prefects willingly perform this office.

When they arrive at the sick man, the priest with a spoon takes out one *margarita* from the *pyxomelum* and pours over it wine brought from the church to soften it. The supplications, exactly according to the Confession of Sins, are recited first by the priest and then by the sick man to whom the priest offers the eucharist. They pray for good fortune and then return with the same pomp as before to replace the *margaritae* in the church.

In the bema, too, although in another place, the oil of consecration is kept in a tin or silver vessel.

XXI

This, then, is a record of the traces[78] of the churches of newer Greece. If I have not preserved it exactly it is because I lack words. It is not the same, however, in all places, especially in the cities where men and women come together at the same time to hear the rite. In many of the nobler temples, certainly there is the distinction that we have already observed. In the narthex, where we have said the more lowly monks remain, the women stand separated from the men. If, as rarely happens, the church has only one door, this leads into the narthex and through this both men and women enter. The men go into the church through the beautiful door. The women remain in their rightful places. If a wall separates them from the ceremony, they hear it through a door or little gates if there are any. If there are galleries, whose walls reach not to the vault but only as high as a man, the upper part of these is secured with lattices. These the Italians call *gelosiae* and through the holes in these the women hear and see what is done.

If the church has many doors so that its interior is clearly visible, then the men enter through the door which leads into the choir, the women through the narthex—if I may use the term. Where there is no narthex the church is partitioned by means of panels. That part immediately in front of the bema is for the men; the side part is given over to the women. If you call this the *gynaeceum*, you will not be far from the mark.[79] They confine themselves to this area so strictly that when the priest distributes the *antidoron* at the doors of the bema, the women have no access to it since they do not mix with the men. Either the priest himself, or the deacon or some other attendant enters the naos and goes to the door in the paneling that separates the men from the women. There he distributes the consecrated bread.

Elsewhere the women are assigned a place in the upper part of the church surrounded on all sides with chancels and reached by flights of stairs used only by the women. They descend unseen by the men and leave the temple by a door accessible to them alone. This is the custom not only of the recent Greeks but taken from most ancient practice as I have read in Clement, Chrysostom, and elsewhere.[80] They offer no explanation why the rites should be different for men and women.

XXII

The ambo is rarely, if ever, used in the church today: the prayers known as the ὀπισθάμβωνοι[81] are recited in the middle of the church. So, too, there is no *skeuophylakion*[82] joined to the church. This was different from the diaconicum which I have described above. However, the priests still carry the sacred vessels and the other church utensils to a special room where they are kept. Monks carry this equipment to the monastery tower or to some fortified place. Not only the valuables of the church and the monastery are brought here but, when necessary, also their own precious goods. In this way they are certain to be safe at such times. You ask why the skeuophylakion, which was a part of the temple, is no longer used. I could in addition tell you more about the porticoes, the *choneuterion*[83] and other lesser parts of the temple, but I do not want to turn this letter into a volume.

XXIII

The Greek mass for the dead is that of John Chrysostom and recited on festivals and other days. However, it differs in that the Epistle and the Gospel are read at that time and frequently a μερίδα for the dead man is added after the commemoration of the saints. When *collyba*[84] are used the rite is solemnly performed. Many candles are lighted, quite often by the priest himself and the panegyric, if I may call it so, is protracted a long time with supplication to God for the soul of the deceased and with blessing of the oblation. When the collyba are at last distributed, wine is often poured into the cups of the assembly. Thus the memory of the dead is made dear and as long lasting as possible.[85]

Afterwards the parents and relatives return to the house and dip into the whitest loaves made of the best flour and divided into immense portions. Noble red wine is consumed, mixed with best oil. Drunk with wine and oil they visit their neighbors and the poor, then go home and send baskets of wine to friends and to the needy. However the priest, presiding as though master of these ceremonies, is not served in the general distribution, but chooses the better things for himself and returns home heavily laden. He rejoices not only in the dead but at other times too when he must celebrate masses and become rich with a variety of goods and utensils. Inasmuch as Christians venerate the temple both in their lifetime and in death, they are accustomed to hand over to the priests who say masses for them or their families, money, bread, and wine, sometimes beans, sweets, and other dishes. While the priest officiates at the south altar in the bema, in the parabema, or wherever he may be, these goods are placed beside him and brought to his house after the mass. Often they are heaped so high that his household, already amply supplied, feeds nobly and abundantly.

Again, the women of the Turks more than contend with the Christians in sending the gifts on which the priests are nourished. So that the light before the holy images does not fail whereby they might suffer harm, they give oil for the lamp—secretly, however, and unknown to their husbands and other Turks. Lest you wonder at this liberality, which is far from slight, the priests lead the Turks' sons to wash in the water of the sacred fount and baptize them with chrism. The Greeks anoint their children at the same baptismal ceremony.

XXIV

But what more should I tell Morin about the temples of the recent Greeks, since no one considers these sacred affairs as matters of great importance. I have done what you commanded me and will do in the future whatever you require. I have erred in many things but my compliance with your wishes cannot be faulted. If this pleases you, then it is well. But if not, turn it on your anvil, go over it again, beat it and polish it and put it together in better shape. With the hammer of your prudence and your wisdom, make it so that it will be pleasing, if this can be done without trouble. If I have abandoned this subject in desperate health, then remedy this ruin, o Vulcan, and all will be well. Farewell, my Morin, and continue to love me.

THE SECOND LETTER

TO THE CELEBRATED AND LEARNED JEAN MORIN

I

I HAD WRITTEN TO YOU, most illustrious man, about the temples of the later Greeks and those which Christian faith—at the present time in the direst servitude—has constructed anew, or received from its forebears and preserved: these churches are not the fruit of the extravagant generosity of many, as Christian piety requires. Before I had conceived this idea, expressed perhaps in inaccurate language, your skillful genius and extraordinary industry elegantly represented it in pictures. And now that I may take possession of my concepts with my own eyes,[86] I rejoice since there will be no difficulties and I can apply my mind constantly to my writing. But, if I do not displease my Morin, as may be, I have enough employment for myself beside this work. Am I obliged to return to writing? I comply readily.

II

Before anything else, I must observe that the holy temple of St. Athanasius at Rome is not built according to the custom of the Greek nation,[87] so that it could and should be adduced as an example of their contemporary churches. It presents rather the manner of a Latin church and is not very ancient.[88] Only by its bema is it to be distinguished from Latin churches. But if you except the space between the walls under the vault, it has nothing in common with the churches of the Greeks. The entrance itself is different. It has neither narthex nor portico, nor is the sanctuary separated from the other parts. The altars are hollowed on both sides[89] and the women are not separated from the men by lattices. However, the temple is suitable enough for use by the young in the service of God.

Therefore an idea of the newer temples must be sought from other sources. These, as we have said elsewhere, are made up of three distinct parts: the narthex, the naos, and the bema. In the space between the naos and the bema, the singers and readers have their place, not on another level, part of the bema yet separated from it, but one which extends from the rounded spaces of the sanctuary. This will have been understood from my words—if well expressed, I do not know. It is to be observed best in the temples of St. Clement and St. Athanasius, as my Morin has noted. Without disturbing the choir and causing no hindrance or obstacle, the doors of the sanctuary can be opened; the images on the panels of the bema are exposed to the eyes of all and can be censed without obstructing anyone.

III

But I may be permitted to digress from my proposed subject—truly, however, not for long—before I proceed further. For I have from your pictures, all of which reproduce the unvarying rectangular form of these sacred buildings, the chance that I desired. Nor will I lose it.

The forms of temples, not only the old but the newer temples too, can be reduced to five [*sic*] basic types.[90] The rest are derived from or can be referred to these. They are the τρουλλωτὰ, the κυλινδρωτὰ, the θολωτὰ, and the κυκλοειδή. Nor is there too much difference between them. Other types are the καμαρωτὰ, the σταυρωτὰ, and the δρομικὰ. Still others are mixtures of these.

The τρουλλωτὰ are those which have their highest part "trullate,"[91] that is, those whose vault diminishes in width towards its highest point where it ends in a round arch. This name comes from *trulla—trullon* according to some, *trullos* according to others—which denotes an arch or a vault. Thus the dome of the Great Church built by Justinian and repaired as Codinus relates in his work on the origins of Constantinople.[92] So, too, John Phocas in his invaluable little book about the holy places of Palestine which I have already translated into Latin and am preparing for publication.[93] Zonaras

called the dome σφαῖρα on account of its likeness to a sphere.[94] The dome
was not always constructed of stone but sometimes out of various types of
wood coming together at its center as in a shield. This I learn from Codinus'
book on the origins of Constantinople in Meursius' edition.[95] I would read
κυπαριάσινος instead of κιασάρινος as Meursius does: thus it would be made
of a wood that never rots.[96] A dome of this type we can see built in our own
day in the Trastevere region of Rome: the temple of the Carmelites to the
Holy Virgin.[97]

The trullate type differed very little from the κυλινδρωτὰ which rose
symmetrically from a round base, in the form of a cylinder with equal and
parallel sides; little, too, from the κυκλοειδή which took their name from
their circular shape. They were little different, again, from the θολωτὰ, in
which all the beams customarily came together in the middle of the roof and
were fixed bordering on each other as in a shield or navel. This type might be
called the "tortoise-temple," circular in shape and growing towards a sharp
point. Thus in the great dictionary of Photius[98] and in John Phocas.[99] These
authors refer to smaller buildings similar to those huts where monks or
hermits kept themselves shut up as Palladius describes in his *Historia
Lausiaca*.[100]

The καμαρωτὰ are those churches which end in a vault. They are covered
by archwork and an in-turning roof.[101] If examples are to be found elsewhere,
these are vaulted in a manner similar to those garden pergolas which give
shade to walkers with various kinds of trees and thickets with creeping
shrubs and which rest upon wooden supports. This vault is truly a tortoise,
its highest part being an inclined roof curving in and out in just this fashion.
One may also find other uses of this word: for example, meaning the whole
building, that is the walls and vault taken together. Thus John Phocas in his
work on the temples of Palestine.[102]

The σταύροειδῆ or σταυρωτὰ are churches in the form of a cross with arms
extended on both sides. These divide the part of the church where the altar
is located from that part which leads to the entrance. In this way Cedrenus
describes the Church of the Blachernae[103] and of this sort many are to be seen
in Rome.

The δρομικὰ are churches with a rectangular plan having either equal or unequal sides. At the roof, rafters or beams are held together with purlins[104] and concealed with tiles in such a way that the walls of the temple are covered with projecting beams. How these churches justify their name will not be easy to discover. If I must conjecture, however, I would say that it comes from the expanse of wall above the architraves which stretch from the façade of the temple to the sanctuary. The entire inner space of the temple is traversed in this way. The type derives its name from δρόμος which means a course or a wandering. Thus Codinus on the church of St. Sophia, δρομικῇ τὸ πρότερον οὔσῃ.[105]

The "mixed" churches were an intermingling of these types as Phocas describes.[106]

In the same way, there are different kinds of vaults. Some are curved like tortoises, others as a hemisphere, and still others—a majority—are supported by a good many arches. The composite types Philander, in his book on Vitruvius, calls mixed and uncertain.[107] Thus the different types of temples have considerable variation in their manner of vaulting. But the new temples of the Greeks, since they are not proudly built, can nearly all be seen to be *dromika*. Provided that they are not looked into, they have almost the appearance of private houses.

IV

These *dromika* are barrel-vaulted[108] and enclose a rectangular area in front of the bema. Nor are all sides of equal length but, as the situation requires, are broader in one direction or extended further in another, the length always prevailing over the breadth. *Trullae* and *tholoi* are rare in cities for their splendid appearance would entice the eyes of enemies and excite envy.

I can end this classification of sacred buildings if I may add one type that has already been investigated by others, although I do not know if it has been explained satisfactorily. This is the church with *emboli*. You will find as many explanations of *embolus* as you want among the grammarians and the lexicographers.[109] I see that there were emboli in the forum and in other buildings as Codinus describes in his unpublished work on the origins of Constantinople.[110]

To the Greeks of our day the term signifies nothing but the portico of a church. The part is certainly that built in front of the door of sacred buildings with a variety of posts linked together[111] and covered with tiles. This offers shelter from the discomforts of the heat and sudden showers, agreeable shade and a pleasant promenade. Its name comes from ἐμβάλλω, since the entrance opens through this portico. Others say that emboli are so called either because they are enclosed or because one walks under them, as beneath the street porticoes which are to be found everywhere. These will be familiar to everyone.

On Chios and elsewhere I have myself seen churches with a similar portico not only at the front but also on one or both of its flanks.[112] But these were a little lower, as though the site were surrounded by a wall and the entire temple shut in with a fortification. In this way, one could go around the entire church all the while concealed from view. If the building is quite low, a series of beams from the ridge curves over the roof on to stone or brick piers or cement walls. These piers frequently rest on floors paved with brick or tile. Where the slope falls away, a small wall, as high as a man's navel, runs around a walk planted with trees to protect it from mud and flood waters. If the building is higher, the beams come not from its roof but from a level which the builder has judged more satisfactory. It may be a structure such as can be seen today in Rome on your right as you enter the hospital of Santo Spirito di Sassia.

Yet this is different from the Greek building which I describe. The walls inside the Roman church are all covered with the smoothest possible marble: on this bare surface, nothing is represented. But in Greek churches the walls are full of pictures. With no little skill, they set before the spectator images of saints and offer for his contemplation historical events and six hundred other things. So that the obscurity of their subject-matter and uncertainty about their content does not disturb the spectator, the scene is made known to the reader by a brief description. A single word indicates the name of the saint represented. Thus no moment elapses without some gain in piety. These sparks of faith gradually insinuate their way into the mind and since there is nothing to dispute them, they are confirmed and strengthened.

Such was the embolus of the Great Church where the acts of the Eighth Synod were defined;[113] and so, too, the Carian embolus built at Blachernae by the Emperor Maurice in the fourth year of his reign.[114]

V

You ask where the *solea*[115] is located. Unless all conjecture fails, it was close to the bema and the ambo. Codinus tells us that it was made of gold, and in his *Origins* that it was adorned with silver by Justin, the successor of Justinian.[116] What then is the solea? All the later Greeks say that they do not know. Meursius, as ignorant as they, says that it is the chair of state (*solium*) or throne. This does not satisfy Gretser in his commentary on Codinus.[117] That it was something other than this Curopalates and Cantacuzenus indicate sufficiently clearly: διέρχεσθαι τὸν σωλέαν, to cross the solea,[118] and εἰσέρχεσθαι τὸν σωλέαν, to enter the solea.[119] These statements cannot be reconciled with its being a chair or throne. If you ask Gretser what it is, he will reply that it was a place beside the bema or tabernacle facing the rising sun. That it was the choir is even more improbable and with this latter explanation I will not delay. As to Gretser's answer, there must have been six hundred other places beside the bema which were not the solea. Would it have been that pavement in front of the sanctuary, or a part of it, or that other raised part within the choir? I do not think so. It is fruitless to be told by Curopalates or Cantacuzenus that the Emperor crossed the solea to enter the sanctuary, since he could not do so even if he wished except through the solea; or that the Patriarch who stood in front of the chancels of the bema arrived at that pavement, since the pavement covers the entire area.

Again, the precious material out of which the solea was made does not permit me to believe that it was a part of the pavement trodden by the feet of all; nor that the solea was fine dust fallen on the ground from the crumbling of the solid material in the dome. This does not happen easily to overhanging or fixed parts of the building but rather to those which carry a great load.

Therefore the opinion of Meursius seems more likely and the arguments which Gretser brings against it prove nothing. What should prevent us saying "cross the solea" and "enter the solea" even if it is a throne? For whatever part is relinquished can be said to have been crossed and if you have left it on the left side, from the point of view of the congregation, you can be said to have entered it. But I seek for one fact that is certain about the solea. Moreover, the temples of the Greeks, as they now are, are distinguished by their level, uniform ground, although in some—at the altar or at the entrance—one ascends by means of a few or more than a few steps. Symeon of Thessalonica also mentions the solea in his work against heretics.[120] But the meaning of the word cannot be interpreted from this passage. Would that something occur at some time to explain to us the way in which the term was used!

VI

The parabema is easily understood provided that you attach an altar to the walls and reduce the seats to a more lowly form. This place does not have stalls as in the choir, pleasingly and skilfully made, but a plain board attached to the wall or supported on wooden feet. It has benches, too, of no specific type, which provide a seat for those who want it. It had escaped me, what you learnedly suggest, that in some temples the altar is separated from the πρόθεσις by a wall. However, there is often an opening in this and the wall hardly separates it from the main altar.

Offering no very accurate picture of the temple, I have said that the vault of the sanctuary is longer than it is broad. But this fact may tell us about the new piety of the Greeks. The vault fits the sanctuary rather than rounds it off in a hemisphere drawn with compasses: so much so that frequently no round figure can contain the sanctuary and the choir as equal halves.[121]

The length and size of the choir, and of the narthex, remain to be described. These adhere to no particular measure but rather fit their situation. Thus when the sanctuary is broad and ample, so is the narthex. No one minds if he must stay in the narthex while most men push their way into the choir. During the solemn rite of the divine liturgy, when troops of men flow in to fill all parts of the church, laymen do not enter the gates of the sanctuary in great numbers. On other days the interior is roomy enough for the number in the neighborhood so that no disturbance of the peace occurs.

Not only novices but all laymen too stay in the nartheces of the monasteries. In a convent where admittance is granted to the laity, the women stay with the nuns, the laymen with others of their kind in the choir. If the space is unable to hold so great a crowd, the women go to the higher parts of the building and to upper chambers, if there are any, in the walls and on the various stories. In this way most women have an excellent, unobstructed view.

In the parish churches, the churches of the people, the women use the narthex. The men, who are not always present, stand in the choir with the priests and other clergy. In rural churches, often quite small and scattered here and there among the fields, there is no difference between choir and narthex. Rather everyone, both men and women, is enclosed in one little place. The women occupy one part, the men the other if this can be arranged conveniently. If not, the majority of them are disposed in this manner. When, as often happens, feasts and solemn anniversaries are attended by large numbers of men and women, the women for the most part hear the rite from outside the doors of the church.

In the temple on Chios known as the Campana, where the people frequently congregate in large numbers, the nartheces extend far beyond the flanks of the church.[122] The women go into the narthex by the side door and remain there. The men, if they enter, seek a place inside the naos. If the women go in by the main door which faces the altar and the bema, they immediately reverence the sanctuary and willingly hasten into the narthex for its entrance is not far from the door which stands open on both sides.[123]

Even when people come and go in great numbers, in this constant crush of humanity the rule of position is not offended against since the women indeed stay in the narthex and the men in the naos. Thus, in the parishes, the better-born and more notable people respect the practices of their ancestors from whom they have inherited these well-merited privileges. The wives of the priests keep to their rightful place according to their rank—the wife of the celebrant first and, following her, the more distinguished women. And each of these places is energetically defended against newcomers and transmitted,

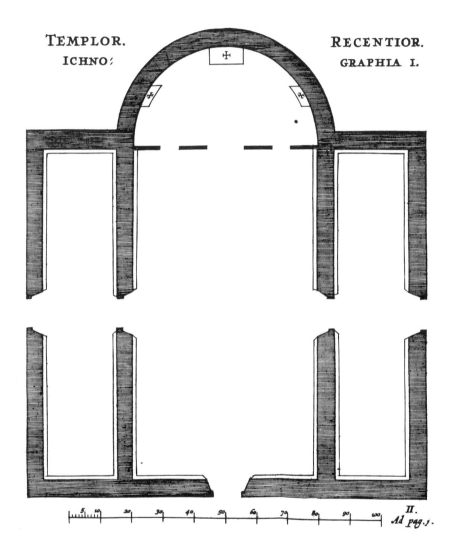

TEMPLOR.   RECENTIOR.
ICHNO: GRAPHIA I.

Fig. 2. Leo Allatios, *De templis Graecorum recentioribus*
(Cologne, 1645), plate II (*photo:* Emory University
Library).

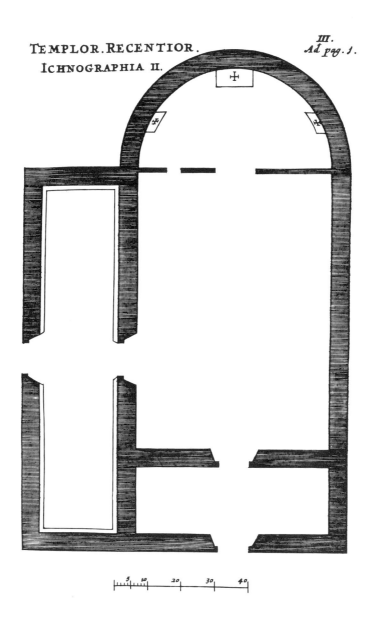

Fig. 3. Leo Allatios, *De templis Graecorum recentioribus*
(Cologne, 1645), plate III (*photo:* Emory University
Library).

I repeat, by law of inheritance to their children. This means that everyone always participates in the rite in the same church and, unless compelled by rare necessity, does not go elsewhere. For if they go to another church they sit in a more despised place, unless they are given a place by some kind possessor of a more dignified seat. This nearly always happens when the newcomer possesses some obvious rank.

In the older parishes, as we have said, the better-born people have places to themselves and seats which they guard as their own. The best place is that to the right upon entering, when the back is turned to the main door, looking directly at the sanctuary. Less noble is that which is behind; and so on for the other seats.

I have always seen one main portal without any side door. The side doors can be anywhere.[124] These would be the παραπόρτια which I freely confess I have not seen. For beside one main door on the façade and another on one side of the naos, I do not remember any third door which, by reason of its position, might open on to the sanctuary. And yet, where a convenient entrance in the flanks of the temple cannot be provided for the women, a little door is opened in the side leading not to the sanctuary but directly into the narthex. This narthex is very often separated from the church by paneling or commonly by a brick or cement wall somewhat less than the height of a man. Thus the standing women may look into the temple and hear the rite clearly. Above these panels are wooden lattices which conceal the women from the eyes of the men.

VII

Certain parecclesia are attached to the wall of the church, not at a pre-determined place but rather as the builder chooses or for convenience of location. Others are more distant and many are scattered among the other buildings of the monastery. In those which are attached to the church, one enters sometimes through the church, sometimes through the wall of the parecclesium outside the church; when the parecclesia are free-standing they have their own door.

In some monasteries there are as many parecclesia as there are days in the week. In these, except on Sundays and on the feast-days of saints when it is required of all monks to attend the services, one of the monks to whom the duty falls, and who is called the ἑβδομαδάριος, celebrates the rite—one day in one parecclesium, the next day in another. In this way by the time a week has passed, he has celebrated in as many parecclesia. Then the duty of celebrating falls to another hebdomadary and he starts anew. When the liturgy is celebrated in one parecclesium, the others are silent. When these buildings are not attached to the main church, in comparison with which they are very small, the week is usually begun in the parecclesium nearest to the main temple. Or, if they wish, they may begin at another instead of this.

VIII

Some of the chairs or seats in the church are fixed and immobile, others mobile and portable. The portable seats are those not designated as fixed places for some personage but are brought out by seat attendants as the need arises.

Sitting in one of these in the middle of the church, the high priest[125] puts on the sacred vestments before he performs the rite of the mass. Here he remains seated until the Isodus[126] when he enters the bema. Again, when the high priest advances someone to the holy order, chairs are placed beside the beautiful door, or before the altar when there is no ἱερὸν σύνθρονον[127] in the church. Here he sits during the ordination. Again I note from my unpublished euchologion that they are placed in front of the bema during the consecration of a bishop. At Rome, too, one or more of these portable seats are placed in the south part of the church depending on the number of priests to be seated. They sit here while the sacred rites are conducted.

The fixed seats are attached to the wall and cannot ever be moved from this place. Outside of the bema, they are hewn out of wood and fashioned with extraordinary skill. Those who sit here are called the σύνθρονοι, either because they occupy those seats at the same time as others do the benches or because many priests sit here as one body.[128]

In these seats the hierarch[129] sits, visible to all while the rite is performed.

The rest of the clergy sit on both sides of the church, some of them on the lower benches. If there are many bishops present lower in seniority and rank than the bishop of the church, the first bishop among them claims the seat to the right of the local bishop. The rest sit in front of the clergy on other seats. If the bishops present rank above the local bishop, the latter yields the throne and the more eminent take the higher place.

However, it is done otherwise in the Church of Constantinople, although even there not without disturbances and quarrelling. The clergy of this church preside over metropolitans and bishops. Therefore, apart from the few almost equal in rank with the Patriarch, they occupy seats at the temple's entrance and look upon his eminence from afar.

There are other seats in the middle of the bema, behind the altar and nearly always made of stone. This synthronon is aptly described in my euchologion. Since it is different from that other synthronon in front of the bema, this bench is called the ἱερὸν σύνθρονον, the sacred synthronon.

Note in passing the euchologion's very accurate description of Greek altars. The slab is made of stone and supported at its angles by four columns, although sometimes by a single pedestal in the middle. Everything beneath it is therefore open and visible to all. Sometimes the altar rests on a solid base of stone, brick, or cement. When it is supported by columns, a chest in the pavement holds the relics of saints. When it is solid there is an orifice in the base which, after closing, because of the structure's uniformity, is not easily distinguished. This orifice is located in the rear part of the altar looking towards the east—that is, opposite the synthronon—or else between its two eastern columns facing away from the church.

IX

After consecration the bishops are carried to the sacred synthronon, so that they may know that their acts are possessed of authority as if they were seated on the throne of majesty;[130] and the sermon from the sacred synthronon is kept among the pastophoria in the sacristy.[131] This throne is considered as the highest of dignities and marks of honor. From it and from what is done on this throne, the summit of eminence, comes the name of the principal rank in the Church, in the same way as honor comes to the holy order of priests from the name of the bema.[132] Nor could this rank be better expressed in any other way. Thus we say the throne of Constantinople, the throne of Jerusalem, of Alexandria, of Antioch, and so on.

X

I have written this second letter to you, most illustrious man, about the newer temples of the Greeks, that I might respond to some doubtful propositions. I have yielded to your authority and your great and undeviating zeal for knowledge. I will do so again in the future if you command me. And I stress this before all else, that in the future nothing that is commanded by you will ever seem laborious to me. Farewell, and continue to love me.

Rome, 5 October 1643

NOTES

NOTES

1. Allatios uses the Vitruvian term *contignatio* (1.15 ; 2.9) in a variety of senses. Depending on the context it can mean flooring, joist, storey, etc.
2. *Descriptio constitutionis monasterii Studii* 2 (*Patrologia Graeca* 99, col. 1704D). Cf. A. Dimitrievski, "The Monastery Rules of St. Saba" (in Russian), *Trudi Kievskoj duch. akad.,* I (1890), pp.170–92.
3. *Iambi de variis argumentis,* 10 (*P.G.* 99, col. 1784).
4. On Mount Athos and elsewhere there are often two forms of summons to the liturgy—the *sēmantron* made of wood and the *sidēroun* made of iron. The latter is sounded as a second warning ten minutes after the *sēmantron*. Cf. P. de Meester, *Voyage de deux Bénédictins aux monastères du Mont-Athos* (Paris, 1908), p. 175.
5. *Meditatum de convocatione . . . per tria signa* (*P.G.* 138, cols. 1073–5).
6. *Hist.,* ed. I. Bekker, II (Bonn, 1835), p. 19.
7. A different objection to bells—that they attracted evil spirits—is recorded by H. H. Jessup, *The Women of the Arabs* (London, 1874), p. 304, and by Mrs. Mackintosh, *Damascus and its People* (London, 1883), p. 31. That bells kept away angels was a widespread Muslim belief. Cf. F. W. Hasluck, *Christianity and Islam under the Sultans,* Vol. I (Oxford, 1929), p. 189, n. 1.
8. See n. 5.
9. Cf. Sir Paul Rycaut, *The Present State of the Greek and Armenian Churches, Anno Christo 1678* (London 1679), p. 220: "In no parts of *Turkie,* or Dominions of the G. Signor, unless in *Moldavia, Wallachia* and Mount *Athos* are Bells permitted."
10. Rycaut, *ibid.,* p. 261, provides further explanation: "In every monastery they have Bells. Such as they daily use are small, but those of greatest bigness are about 4 or 500 weight, which they ring at Festivals, when they would make the greatest noise and rejoicing: on these their Clocks strike, which are fixed like those on our Churches in England; which are not to be found, as I remember, in any other place in *Turkey,* unless at *Buda,* where I saw one of this sort."
11. *Sc.* both bells and *vareae* are made of brass.
12. In addition to the two signals described in n. 4, *supra,* a third was given with a bell. This was not pealed. Rather the clapper was struck against the side of one bell, while the others were oscillated rapidly.
13. *In can. 45 Beat. Patr. qui Carth. convenerunt* (*P.G.* 138, col. 173D).
14. *Hist. compend.,* ed. I. Bekker, Vol. I (Bonn, 1839), p. 679. Allatios does not explain the significance of the *garsonostasion* as a waiting place for servants. This is explained in J. Goar's notation, *ibid.,* Vol. II, p. 805, and by Du Cange, *Glossarium ad scriptores*

mediae et infimae Graecitatis, col. 238: "Garsonostasion sic appellatum Atrium subdiale ante aedem Sophiam Constantinopoli in quo scilicet consistebant procerum famuli, quos Garcones . . . Graeci vocabant." Cf. R. Janin, *Constantinople byzantine* (Paris, 1964), p. 353.

15. *Hist.,* ed. I. Bekker (Bonn, 1835), p. 106. Choniates uses the word ὄικος which Allatios translates as *templum.*

16. See pp. 30–31.

17. Cf. Symeon of Thessalonica, *De sacro ordine sepulture,* cap. 364 (*P.G.* 155, col. 677D).

18. That is, penitents of the first class. Cf. Tertullian, *De poenitentibus,* cap. 7 (*P.G.* 1, col. 1352).

19. Νάρθηξ λέγεται ὅπου ἁι γυναῖκες ἐν τῷ ἱερῷ ἵστανται. I have been unable to verify this quotation.

20. Curopalates, *De officiis Constantinopolitanis,* 15 (*P.G.* 157, 97D).

21. See n. 9, *supra.*

22. *Vita S. Pauli iunioris, Analecta Bollandiana,* Vol. XI (1892), p. 165. Allatios employs this same quotation in his *De rebus ecclesiasticis Graecorum* (Paris, 1646), p. 117.

23. Cf. Acts 5, p. 16.

24. Curopalates, *De officiis,* cap. 17 (*P.G.* 157, col. 105D).

25. The royal (literally imperial) doors, a term also applied to the central door of the bema screen. For Allatios' understanding of the disposition of these several doors, see Fig. 1. Cf. Pseudo-Codinus, *De officiis,* ed. J. Verpeaux (Paris, 1966), p. 268, l. 23.

26. In later Greek churches it is the side doors of the iconostasis that are called "angelic." Customarily they carry icons of angels, sometimes the image of a deacon holding his *orarion* and making a gesture of prayer.

27. Allatios uses the word *rector.*

28. More aptly because the term *stasidion* preserves the sense of support for those who stand. In the early Christian church, clerics and monks remained standing but leaned on a crutch, for which the *stasidion* became the medieval substitute.

29. *Med.,* 668.

30. *Od.,* 1, 50.

31. *Pyth.,* 4, 74.

32. Balsamon, *In. can. 74 Conc. in Trullo.* (*P.G.* 137, col. 765D).

33. This chamber, to the south of the sanctuary, houses the sacred vessels and vestments in care of the deacons. In earlier Greek writers, e.g., Theophanes, *Chronographia,* ed. J. Classen (Bonn, 1839), 120, 14, it is often called σκευοφυλακεῖον, sacristy.

34. Allatios notwithstanding, this limitation is imposed in the 19th canon, *Select Library of Nicene and Post-Nicene Fathers,* ed. P. Schaff and H. Wace (New York, 1900), p. 136.

35. *Ibid.,* p. 396.

36. *In. can. 69 Conc. in Trullo.* (*P.G.* 137, col. 752). The prohibition against women probably derives from Leviticus 15.

37. *Ibid.,* cols. 752–3.

38. The force of this particular argument is not clear.

39. See n. 37.

40. The earliest account of this exchange is to be found in Theodoretus, *Eccles. hist.,* 17 (*P.G.* 82, col. 1232).

41. 7, 24–5 (*P.G.* 72, cols. 1494–6).

42. *Eccles. hist.,* 12, 41 (*P.G.* 145, cols. 889–97).
43. The theory and practice of the imperial entry into the bema is discussed by O. von Simson, *Sacred Fortress* (Chicago, 1948), pp. 27–39.
44. Cf. Curopalates, *De officiis,* 17 (*P.G.* 157, col. 109B) and Cantacuzenus, *Hist.,* ed. L. Schopen, Vol. I (Bonn, 1828), p. 198; also p. 8.
45. The Greek ecclesiastical book most frequently drawn on by Allatios in the writing of this and other works. This type of prayer-book contains the complete text of the sacraments together with the Ritual for monastic use, for the burial of the dead, for the consecration of the church, etc. We have no means of knowing the precise text of Allatios' copy. It was certainly a manuscript, for he frequently describes his euchologion as *nondum editus.* The most important seventeenth century version printed in the west was that edited by Jacques Goar (Paris, 1644). This edition, reprinted at Venice in 1730, is informed by a thorough and critical use of patristic and Byzantine texts.
46. A corruption of βηλόθυρον to be found for instance in Curopalates, *De officiis,* ed. I. Bekker (Bonn, 1839), p. 49. Patristic writers, such as Gregory Nazianzen, use the word *katapetasma,* the term used in the New Testament (e.g., Mark 15:38) and the Septuagint (e.g., Exodus 26:31) for the veil of the holy of holies.
47. A traditional name for the bema. Cf. Procopius, *De aed.,* 1, 4, 2.
48. The altar or altar part of the sanctuary. Cf. Septuagint, Genesis 8:20; Matthew 23:18; Procopius, 3, col. 2836C.
49. Originally the mercy-seat, the cover of the ark. Cf. Septuagint, Exodus 25:16–22; Philo. 2, 150, 2.
50. Cf. Nicetas Choniates, *Hist.,* ed. I. Bekker (Bonn, 1835), p. 631.
51. *Orat.* 43 (*P.G.* 36, col. 532C).
52. Cf. Du Cange, *Glossarium,* col. 196.
53. Allatios latinizes the Greek term *anagnostai.*
54. The *prothesis* is, strictly, not a side altar but a sort of credence table used in the rite of preparation.
55. The *antidoron* consists of particles of bread distributed by the priest to the congregation after the communion. It is the remainder of the bread from which the priest has first cut the *amnos,* which serves as the principal host, and then the *prosphora,* particles in honor of the Mother of God and the saints. Cf. the early ninth century description by Gregorius Decapolita (*P.G.* 100, col. 1204) and Rycaut (*op. cit.,* pp. 177–81) on the Greek sacrament in the seventeenth century and Pseudo-Codinus, *De officiis,* ed. J. Verpeaux (Paris, 1966), p. 268, l. 23. On the form and meaning of the Byzantine *prothesis,* see M. Mandalà, *La protesi della liturgia nel rito bizantino* (Grottaferrata, 1935).
56. Jacob Gretser, Swiss Jesuit scholar (1562–1625). His collected works were published at Ratisbon, 1734–1741, and include the commentary on Codinus which is included in I. Bekker's edition of this author (Bonn, 1843).
57. Cf. Joannes Malalas, *Chron.,* ed. L. Dindorf (Bonn, 1831), p. 457.
58. On the changing functions of the diaconicum, see J. Lassus, *Sanctuaires chrétiens de Syrie* (Paris, 1947), pp. 194 ff.
59. *Hyperetēs* signifies a servant in the church, a minister below the rank of *anagnostēs.* Cf. *Select Library of Nicene and Post-Nicene Fathers,* ed. P. Schaff and H. Wace, Vol. XIV (New York, 1900), p. 140.

60. *Ibid.*
61. Allatios obviously had access to several manuscripts of the Laodicean canons. His emendation would substitute "in attendance" or "at the service" for "in the diaconicum."
62. *Sancti Artemisii Passio* (P.G. 96, col. 1272C).
63. *Eccles. hist.*, 1 (P.G. 86, col. 188B).
64. In Curopalates, *De officiis*, ed. I. Bekker (Bonn, 1839), p. 62, a tablecloth. Many varieties of spelling occur, usually as a neuter noun. Cf. *De ceremoniis*, ed. J. Reiske (Bonn, 1829), p. 465 and Theophanes Cont., *Chron.*, ed. I. Bekker (Bonn, 1838), p. 661.
65. In Theophanes, *Chron.*, ed. J. Classen (Bonn, 1839), p. 697, a portable altar. Again, with orthographical variation, in Curopalates, *De officiis*, ed. I. Bekker (Bonn, 1839), 5, a consecrated tablecloth. For the complex history of the *antimension*, see G. A. Rhalles and M. Potles, Σύνταγμα των θείων και ιερων κανόων κτλ., 5 (Athens, 1852–1859), pp. 413–14.
66. Xylander was the hellenized name of Wilhelm Holtzmann (1532–1576), the classical philologist responsible for the first German translation of Euclid. Despite his painstaking commentary on Cedrenus, reprinted in I. Bekker's edition (Bonn, 1839), the Protestant scholar is roundly rebuked as a heretic in Allatios' next sentences.
67. The Office of the Prothesis is now a special preparatory service in the Greek rite.
68. A description of the symbolic act of severing the *amnos* (the Lamb), the central part of the host from the rest of the bread which is used as the *prosphora* and *antidoron*. Cf. p. 16, n. 55, *supra*.
69. Allatios uses the Latin word *patina* rather than the Greek *diskos*.
70. The *merides* are fragments of the bread set apart for the Mother of God, the saints and for all Orthodox Christians living or dead.
71. *P.G.* 63, col. 915.
72. *Paedagogus*, 2, 12 (P.G. 8, col. 540C).
73. *Iambi de variis argumentis*, 42 (P.G. 99, col. 1293C).
74. Literally, a casket for the consecrated bread. The tabernacle in which the casket is kept is called by the same name.
75. The sponge represents that filled with vinegar and given to Christ on the Cross (Matthew 27:48).
76. *P.G.* 63, col. 920. On the *mousa*, cf. Du Cange, *Glossarium*, col. 963, an entry obviously dependent on Allatios' observation here.
77. This is confirmed for Chios by Jean Dumont, a French visitor of 1694, quoted in P. P. Argenti and S. P. Kyriakidis, 'Η Χιος παρὰ τοῖς γεωγράφοις καὶ περιηγηταῖς, Vol. I (Athens, 1946), p. 498. Dumont also asserts that the Chiots were permitted to use bells in their churches.
78. Allatios uses the word *ichnographia*, presumably aware that Morin would understand it in its etymological sense rather than with the simpler meaning of 'plan' already current in the early seventeenth century.
79. Cf. Procopius, *De aed.*, 1, 1, 58.
80. Clement, *Constit. Apost.*, 2, 57 (P.G. 1, col. 732), Chrysostom, *In Matthaeum homil.*, 63 (P.G. 58, col. 677).
81. The *eukhē opisthambonos* is a prayer which the priest says at the end of the liturgy standing "behind the ambo" in the middle of the choir.

82. The treasury or sacristy of a church (or palace). Cf. Theophanes, *Chron.*, ed. I. Bekker (Bonn, 1838), p. 120.
83. A sink, usually in the sanctuary, into which ablutions and baptismal water were thrown after use.
84. The *kollyba* is an oblation of boiled wheat distributed to the congregation in remembrance of the dead. Today, rice is usually served for this purpose.
85. The details of these ritual comestibles are confirmed by Rycaut, *op. cit.*, 298.
86. Allatios' language suggests that at some time between the writing of his first and second letter he had received three drawings (figs. 1–3) from Morin. His correspondent apparently asked further questions about Greek architecture and ritual which Allatios attempts to answer in this second letter employing Roman examples such as the Greek College and the upper Church of St. Clement that Morin has probably mentioned.
87. The word *natio* is used here not to describe a political entity which did not exist after 1453, but the Greek *milet*, the organization of the Greek people under its church as required by Muslim tradition. On the *milet* system, see Sir Steven Runciman, "The Greek Church under the Ottoman Turks," *Studies in Church History,* Vol. II (London, 1965), pp. 39–40.
88. The Greek College of St. Athanasius, which admitted non-Catholics but hoped to convert them, was founded by Gregory XIII in 1577.
89. Allatios would seem to contrast this form with the plain slab of stone that since the Constantinian age had served the Greeks for an altar-table. Cf. p. 36.
90. From what follows immediately it will be seen that Allatios does not confine himself to five *summa genera*. On this manner of classification, see cap. 4 of Intro.
91. The author simply latinizes the Greek form and employs it henceforth as a synonym for "domical."
92. Cf. Codinus, *De structura templi S. Sophiae* (*P.G.* 157, col. 629). On the term *troullos,* see R. Janin, *Constantinople byzantine* (Paris, 1964), p. 437.
93. *Descriptio terrae sanctae* (*P.G.* 133, col. 939B). Allatios' preface, describing the manuscripts of Phocas' book is reprinted in this volume of Migne.
94. *Annal.* 14 (*P.G.* 134, col. 1250C).
95. The commentary of Jan de Meurs, Netherlandish philologist (1579-1639), is included in both the editions of Migne and Bekker (Bonn, 1843) and in his collected works, edited by J. Lami (Florence, 1741–1763).
96. *De structura templi Sanctae Sophiae* (*P.G.* 157, col. 625A). Allatios' emendation would substitute cypress for pumice as the structural material of the dome.
97. Santa Maria in Transpontina, begun in 1470 by Meo del Caprino and modified by Bramante and Bernini.
98. *Photii Patriarchae Lexicon,* ed. S. A. Naber, Vol. I (Leyden, 1864), p. 282.
99. *Descriptio terrae sanctae,* cap. 24 (*P.G.* 133, col. 953C). Cf. also *ibid.,* cap. 14 (col. 941B) and cap. 18 (col. 949A).
100. Ed. C. Butler (Cambridge, 1898), cap. 35 (col. 1107C).
101. Presumably a pumpkin dome as over the center bay of the Budrum Čami at Constantinople. Cf. R. Krautheimer, *Early Christian and Byzantine Architecture* (Harmondsworth, 1965), p. 261 and pl. 137B.
102. *Descriptio terrae sanctae* (*P.G.* 133, cols. 941C and 956D).

103. *Hist. compend.,* ed. I. Bekker (Bonn, 1838), p. 684.

104. Purlins=*cantheria.* It is evident from this and other passages that Allatios is both uninterested in and ignorant of roof construction. He uses *asser* and *trabs* as synonyms in such a way that this paragraph is hardly comprehensible from a technical point of view.

105. *De aedificiis Constantinopolitanis (P.G.* 157, col. 548B). Cf. *De structura templi S. Sophiae (P.G.* 157, col. 613A).

106. *Descriptio terrae sanctae,* caps. 15, 22 (*P.G.* 133, cols. 944D, 952D). By the "mixed" type, Allatios might mean a church such as the Brontocheion at Mistra where a basilican plan is blended with that of a cross church with galleries over the transept arms.

107. *G. Philandri in decem Libros M. Vitruvii Pollionis de Architectura Annotationes* (Rome, 1544), 7, 2.

108. *=in semicirculum arcuantur.*

109. On *embolus* as a mechanical term, cf. Vitruvius, 10, 7–12. For the more complex connotations of the term in the 6th century A.D., see G. L. Huxley, *Anthemius of Tralles, a Study in Later Greek Geometry* (Cambridge, Mass., 1959), p. 8. I am indebted to Professor C. L. Striker for an enlightening correspondence about the range of meanings of this term.

110. *De aedificiis Constantinopolitanis (P.G.* 157, col. 609A). Cf. Cyril of Scythopolis, *Vita Sabae,* col. 328C. On the use of porticoes in the Great Palace at Constantinople, see R. Krautheimer, *op. cit.,* pp. 251-3.

111. *=variis asseribus inter se conjunctis.* Allatios presumably refers to the sort of arcaded portico that survives today on the north side of the Church of the Pantanassa at Mistra.

112. No such church is described in either A. C. Orlandos, *Monuments byzantins de Chios* (Athens, 1930) or A. Smith, *The Architecture of Chios,* ed. P. Argenti (London, 1962).

113. Convoked at Constantinople in A.D. 806 by Nicephorus I.

114. Cedrenus, *Hist. compend.,* ed. I. Bekker (Bonn, 1838), p. 694.

115. The threshold of the sanctuary, usually raised a step or two above the choir and adorned with a rich pavement. Sometimes *solea* is understood to refer to the raised pathway from the bema to the ambo as it survives, for instance, in the fourth century church of St. Thecla at Milan. For the term *solea* in the Palaeologan period, see Pseudo-Codinus, *De officiis,* ed. J. Verpeaux (Paris, 1966), p. 260, l. 2; p. 262, l. 1; p. 265, l. 3. J. Goar, *Euchologion . . .* (n. 45, *supra*), points out that the term *solea* was unknown to the Greek and Latin Fathers but otherwise adds nothing to Allatios' discussion. For a modern definition, see F. E. Brightman, *Liturgies Eastern and Western,* Vol. I (Oxford, 1896), p. 583, and cf. S. G. Xydis, "The Chancel Barrier, Solea and Ambo of Hagia Sophia," *Art Bulletin* XXIX (1947), pp. 10 ff.

116. *De structura templi S. Sophiae (P.G.* 157, cols. 625D, 629A). Cf. Curopalates, *De officiis,* 17 (*P.G.* 157, col. 109B).

117. This debate will be found in the Migne edition of Curopalates (*P.G.* 157, col. 402).

118. *De officiis,* 17 (*P.G.* 157, col. 109B).

119. *Hist.,* ed. L. Schopen, Vol. I (Bonn, 1828), p. 198.

120. The citation, which concerns the seating of subdeacons and lector περὶ τὸν σώλεαν is actually to be found in Symeon's *De sacro templo,* cap. 85 (*P.G.* 155, col. 345B).

121. *Sc.* choir and sanctuary do not make up a circle divided in two by the doors of the bema.

122. I have been unable to identify the church to which Allatios specifically refers. But the *katholikon* of the Nea Moni has such an exonarthex, cf. A. C. Orlandos, *Monuments byzantins de Chios,* Vol. II (Athens, 1930), pl. 10. R. Krautheimer, *op. cit.,* pp. 243 and 264, asserts that several later churches on Chios have such a disproportionate narthex but does not identify these.

123. Nothing in Allatios' text serves to resolve the obvious ambiguity of this sentence.

124. Side doors are clearly indicated on the *tabellae* reproduced in Figs. 2 and 3.

125. =*pontifex.*

126. Allatios latinizes the Greek ἔισοδος.

127. The semi-circular bench reserved for the clergy at the back of the apse. This *presbyterium* Allatios distinguishes from the *synthronon* of priests in the nave discussed in the next paragraph.

128. Cf. Eusebius, *Hist. eccles.,* 10, 4 (*P.G.* 20, col. 868c).

129. =antistes, Greek ἱεράρχης.

130. Cf. Clement, *Const. Apost.* (*P.G.* 1, col. 1076A).

131. Ibid., cols. 724–5. In architectural history, the pastophories are rooms flanking the main apse of the church and serving as prothesis or diaconicum. On this feature of the Byzantine church, see R. Krautheimer, *op. cit.,* pp. 69, 183, 284.

132. Cf. p. 13.